"The Object Lessons series achieves something very close to magic: the books take ordinary—even banal—objects and animate them with a rich history of invention, political struggle, science, and popular mythology. Filled with fascinating details and conveyed in sharp, accessible prose, the books make the everyday world come to life. Be warned: once you've read a few of these, you'll start walking around your house, picking up random objects, and musing aloud: 'I wonder what the story is behind this thing?'"

Steven Johnson, author of *Where Good Ideas Come From* and *How We Got to Now*

"Object Lessons describes themselves as 'short, beautiful books,' and to that, I'll say, amen. . . . If you read enough Object Lessons books, you'll fill your head with plenty of trivia to amaze and annoy your friends and loved ones—caution recommended on pontificating on the objects surrounding you. More importantly, though . . . they inspire us to take a second look at parts of the everyday that we've taken for granted. These are not so much lessons about the objects themselves, but opportunities for self-reflection and storytelling. They remind us that we are surrounded by a wondrous world, as long as we care to look."

John Warner, *The Chicago Tribune*

T0205171

" In 1957 the French critic and semiotician Roland Barthes published *Mythologies*, a groundbreaking series of essays in which he analysed the popular culture of his day, from laundry detergent to the face of Greta Garbo, professional wrestling to the Citroën DS. This series of short books, Object Lessons, continues the tradition."

Melissa Harrison, *Financial Times*

" Though short, at roughly 25,000 words apiece, these books are anything but slight."

Marina Benjamin, *New Statesman*

" The Object Lessons project, edited by game theory legend Ian Bogost and cultural studies academic Christopher Schaberg, commissions short essays and small, beautiful books about everyday objects from shipping containers to toast. *The Atlantic* hosts a collection of 'mini object-lessons'. . . . More substantive is Bloomsbury's collection of small, gorgeously designed books that delve into their subjects in much more depth."

Cory Doctorow, *Boing Boing*

OBJECTLESSONS

A book series about the hidden lives of ordinary things.

Series Editors:

Ian Bogost and Christopher Schaberg

Advisory Board:

Sara Ahmed, Jane Bennett, Jeffrey Jerome Cohen, Johanna Drucker, Raiford Guins, Graham Harman, renée hoogland, Pam Houston, Eileen Joy, Douglas Kahn, Daniel Miller, Esther Milne, Timothy Morton, Kathleen Stewart, Nigel Thrift, Rob Walker, Michele White.

In association with

BOOKS IN THE SERIES

whale song

MARGRET GREBOWICZ

Bloomsbury Academic
An imprint of Bloomsbury Publishing Inc

B L O O M S B U R Y
NEW YORK • LONDON • OXFORD • NEW DELHI • SYDNEY

Bloomsbury Academic
An imprint of Bloomsbury Publishing Inc

1385 Broadway
New York
NY 10018
USA

50 Bedford Square
London
WC1B 3DP
UK

www.bloomsbury.com

BLOOMSBURY and the Diana logo are trademarks of Bloomsbury Publishing Plc

First published 2017
Reprinted 2024

© Margret Grebowicz, 2017

Library of Congress Cataloging-in-Publication Data
A catalog record for this book is available from the Library of Congress.

Names: Grebowicz, Margret, 1973- , author.
Title: Whale song / Margret Grebowicz.
Description: New York : Bloomsbury Academic, 2017. | Series: Object lessons |
Includes bibliographical references and index.
Identifiers: LCCN 2017003734| ISBN 9781501329258 (pbk. : alk. paper) | ISBN
9781501329272 (epdf)
Subjects: LCSH: Cetacea–Psychology. | Animal intelligence. | Human-animal
communication–Research. | Animal communication. | Cetacea–Psychological aspects.
Classification: LCC QL737.C4 G734 2017 | DDC 599.5–dc23 LC record available at
https://lccn.loc.gov/2017003734

ISBN: PB: 978-1-5013-2925-8
ePub: 978-1-5013-2926-5
ePDF: 978-1-5013-2927-2

Series: Object Lessons

Cover design: Alice Marwick

Typeset by Deanta Global Publishing Services, Chennai, India
Printed and bound in Great Britain

Certainly it was only too obvious that the ocean had "noticed" us.

STANISŁAW LEM, *SOLARIS*

To C, with nuzz

CONTENTS

1 SONGS

Remember whale song? Me neither. We are far, far away from the quiet age of sail. That's how cetologists Roger Payne and Scott McVay dreamily describe the centuries of maritime culture prior to propellers. In their article, "Songs of Humpback Whales," which appeared on the cover of *Science* magazine in August 1971, they hearken back to quiet seas, where whalers could occasionally hear the sounds of their prey through the wooden hulls of their ships. The hulls acted as amplifiers. "In this noisy century," Payne and McVay write, referring of course to the 20th, "the widespread use of propeller ships and continuously running shipboard generators has made this a rare occurrence."[1]

It was Second World War research into sonar and antisubmarine warfare that made it possible to capture whale sounds underwater, by means of new technologies. Humans began to hear whales again, despite the ship noise, or, since this was a significantly different experience than hearing through a wooden hull, to hear them for the first time. In fact, for the first time in history, humans who had never even been to the seaside could hear the sounds of whales.

At the time that issue of *Science* appeared, most existing recordings were of odontocetes, or toothed whales, like dolphins, orcas, porpoises, belugas, and sperm whales, whose vocalizing consists primarily of clicks, squeals, squeaks, and whistles. Many of those sounds we now know to be a form of sonar called "echolocation," in which high-frequency clicks bounce off objects, allowing whales to "see" their underwater environment in exquisite detail. The rest constitutes communication about which we still know very little.

It wasn't until the recordings of mysticetes, or the giant baleen whales, that it seemed appropriate to refer to whale sounds as "songs." Baleen whales do not echolocate, but instead make low-frequency sounds that serve to communicate over great distances, even passing around obstacles. The sounds happen in repeating patterns, causing researchers to group them with other song-like behavior, like that of birds. But these sounds came to be called songs not only because of structure, but also because of their particular sonic qualities. Unlike toothed whales, the baleens—like blue whales, fin whales, gray whales, right whales, and of course, the majestic humpbacks—have vocal chords. And due to the enormous distances their sounds travel in water, baleen whale songs constitute the largest communication network for any animals, with the exception of humans.[2]

The first humpback recordings came into existence entirely by accident. In the 1950s, Frank Watlington was an engineer working for the US Navy at a top secret listening station in Bermuda, where the United States was listening for Soviet submarines. His job was to record dynamite explosions and, dropping the broadband hydrophone he had created just for this purpose to the great depth of 1,500 feet one day, Watlington happened to catch something he wasn't prepared for.[3] The sounds were actually in his way, the noise on his dynamite recordings.

Amused and intrigued, he played them for folks at a square dancing function, who were among the first humans to hear whale sounds on playback. Watlington didn't know what to do next, so he handed the recoding over to the young Payne and McVay, who had come to Bermuda to study the already very endangered humpbacks on their migration. It was they who "discovered" the humpbacks in the way one discovers a new vocal sensation, by means of something like a demo. Payne subsequently produced Watlington's recordings of humpbacks, as an LP called *Songs of the Humpback Whale*, released in 1970.[4]

Songs of the Humpback Whale became one of the most important aural documents of the modern environmental movement. It was central to the Save the Whales campaign, whose originator, Christine Stevens, appeared before the US Congress during the Marine Mammal Protection Act debates, and literally rested her case by playing the album.[5] In Stockholm that same year, 1972, the United Nations Conference on the Human Environment resulted in the beginning of global bans on commercial whaling.

The Stockholm Conference was the first time that the United Nations declared environmental damage as a global phenomenon to be addressed collectively by nations, and the moratorium on whaling, proposed by the United States on the heels of its Marine Mammal Protection Act, was adopted by total consensus, a vote of 52-0.[6] In 1975, Greenpeace played *Songs* during their first ever action at sea, during which they confronted a Soviet whaling vessel and blasted the recording over a loudspeaker. Over ten million copies of *Songs* were inserted into the January 1979 issue of *National Geographic*, making this the largest single pressing of any album of recorded music.[7] In 1982, the International Whaling Commission instituted a global ban on all commercial whaling, which went into effect in 1986 and holds to this day.

Given how extensively the world had depended on whale bodies as raw material just decades before, with the baleens providing us the equivalent of plastic well into the second half of the twentieth century, and whale oil lighting the streets of our biggest cities, the banning of whale hunting marks what political scientist Charlotte Epstein calls "one of the most dramatic cases of complete turnabout with regard to a natural resource, and a fundamental restructuring of the resource base of our economies."[8] Blue whales had been declared endangered decades before Greenpeace came onto the scene, but this hadn't stopped humans from hunting them all the more committedly. In the late 1950s killer whales in the North Atlantic were favorite targets for the US Air Force, and *Time* magazine printed a story which featured the following description of such an operation, in which "seventy nine bored GIs responded with enthusiasm" to the invitation to kill orcas: "First the killers [whales] were rounded up in tight formation with concentrated machine gun fire, then moved out again one by one, for the final blast which would kill them. . . . As one was wounded, the others would set upon it and tear it to pieces with their jagged teeth."[9] *Time* did not receive a single dissenting letter upon publication of this article, which makes the fact that "a little over a decade later, such actions would have been made the object of federal prosecution" indeed remarkable.

But whale song had impact well beyond the politics of killing whales. Humpback vocalizations, which Payne described as "the most evocative, most beautiful sounds made by any animal on Earth," in a recent NPR interview, are currently hurtling through interstellar space on the *Voyager Golden Record*, among the most important bits of information that humans in 1977 wished to communicate to whatever alien intelligences might intercept them in the distant future. It will be 40,000 years before they make a close approach to any other planetary system. As Carl Sagan, the curator of the *Golden Record*'s content, meticulously explains, "Each Voyager spacecraft has a golden phonograph record in a silvery aluminum cover affixed to the outside of its central instrument bay. Instructions for playing the record, written in scientific language, are etched on the cover. A cartridge and stylus, illustrated on the cover, are tucked into the spacecraft nearby. The record is ready to play."[10]

The songs are included as part of the "Human and Whale Greetings" section, in which "Hello" appears in sixty human languages spoken by UN delegates, as well as one whale language, humpback. "So as to leave no hint of provincialism in the greetings from the UN delegations, we mixed these characteristically human greetings with the characteristic 'Hellos' of the humpback whale—another intelligent species from the planet Earth sending greetings to the stars."[11] Whales fill a completely different function than birds, which are part of the "Sounds of Earth" track, or Chuck Berry, who appears on the music track. They're included as speakers, somewhere in between humans and the alien intelligences we imagined must be out there. Whaliens.

Humpback songs were so far at the front of Sagan's thinking about *Voyager* that he poetically described the whole *Golden Record* itself as a kind of whale song: "It is, as much as the sounds of any baleen whale, a love song cast upon the vastness of the deep."[12] Whale song seemed to belong as much to a forgotten Earth in need of conservation, a quiet age of sail living only in the annals of human memory, as it did to Cold War technoscience, the search for extraterrestrial life, and a future in which we would be remembered by alien listeners long after we were gone. It came from elsewhere and was destined still elsewhere—haunted, distant, endangered, prehistoric, futuristic, transient, astro-nautical, exiled, extra terrestrial, a sound at the very edge of personhood, speech, music, life, habitat, "Earth," but squarely in the sweet spot of longing.

As the Cold War drew to an end and new legislation allowed whale populations to return to more sustainable numbers, whale song began to slowly recede in the public imagination. In 1986 film *Star Trek IV: The Voyage Home* was still triumphantly humpback-themed. Kirk and Spock travel back in time, from 2286 to 1986, in order to save Earth from destruction by a mysterious probe emitting an indecipherable signal that has disabled the planet's power grid and is causing massive storms. Spock determines that the probe's signal matches the songs of humpback whales, which are long since extinct. With Kirk, he travels to 1986 San Francisco to find a pair of living whales and, in a feat of imagination and physics that seems to take the spirit of *Voyager*'s "Human and Whale Greetings" to something like a logical conclusion, they transport the whales forward in time to 2286. The humpbacks answer the probe's call and save Earth and all its inhabitants from total and certain destruction.

Despite the happy ending, however, this film's mournful dedication points to the impending shift in cultural climate: it was for the astronauts who had died in the Challenger disaster just months before the film's release, a disaster that marked the beginning of the end of NASA's space shuttle program. Meanwhile, NGOs like Greenpeace became serious interlocutors in international environmental politics rather than anti-government radicals. Gradually, whale song went the way of crystals, incense, and new age music dripping with synth and reverb. To quote David Rothenberg, a philosopher and musician who records himself improvising along with humpbacks he hears in real time through a hydrophone, today whale song is shelved with "past lives, weekend shamans, suburban yogis, and other fragments of our yearning for deeper meaning. All of this is easier to dismiss as woo woo than to take seriously."[13] Remember whale song? Me neither.

And yet, as Epstein provocatively suggests, the anti-whaling movement and the subsequent growth of a culture of caring about whales was never just about the welfare of whales. The passion for whales, along with its twin passion, the one for alien intelligences, had everything to do with how people imagined life on Earth and a future of different, better social relations. Whale welfare spread like wildfire because we understood, on some level, that human welfare was at stake.

The first humpback whale recordings thus serve as a strange and delicate document, not only of the songs themselves, but also of a particular moment in human culture. The dramatic shift in attitude to the whale-loving one we now take for granted resulted from changes not in how humans think about whales but in how they think about each other. And at the center of this shift was the question of communication.

2 LONELINESS

In 2013, just as Voyager left the solar system carrying Watlington's humpback sounds into dry, dark, silent interstellar space, whale song reentered the public imagination in a new way: a blue whale became a social media phenomenon. Nicknamed The World's Loneliest Whale, 52 Blue is a migrating blue, probably male, singing at 52 hertz, a frequency too high to be heard by other blue whales or fin whales (there is speculation about him being a blue-fin whale hybrid).

First recorded in 1992, 52 Blue was introduced to the world in 2004, in a scientific article summing up all the trackings of his migration patterns, but became a star almost ten years later, when the popular media began pushing the story, never confirmed by scientists, that his plaintive song was a mating call that would never be answered. The public's imagination caught fire. Indie pop songs have been written about him (Laura Ann Bates's "The Loneliest Creature on Earth" and "The Loneliest Whale in the World" by Dalmatian Rex and the Eigentones), as well as a children's book, Agnieszka Jurek's *52 Hertz Wal*. People have appeared on social media as 52 Blue, setting up Facebook pages and Twitter accounts in his name, with posts that call out to others who aren't there: "Hellooooooo?! Yooohoooooo! Is anyone out there? #SadLife" and "I'm so lonely.:'(#lonely #ForeverAlone."[1]

The latest research continues to point away from the loneliness narrative, arguing that anomalous whale calls are not that unusual, and that there are probably many whales in the same situation as 52. He may happen to be traveling solo, but this is probably not unique, and therefore less tragic than we imagine. The sounds may also be produced by a group of hybrid whales rather than one individual, since we have yet to actually see *the* 52 Blue. But these findings have done little to alter one of the most poignant narratives of social loss today.

As scientists gently suggest that there may be nothing here to talk about, the Web continues to generate ever more articles, like this year's "The Heartbreaking Story of the World's Loneliest Whale," which describes a creature that "roams the world's largest ocean, year after year, desperately calling out for a mate but never finding one."[2] Filmmaker Josh Zeman and actor Adrian Grenier, star of the series *Entourage*, have teamed up to make a documentary, which they have successfully crowdsourced. At the heart of their Kickstarter campaign is the lovely soundbite that it is not a fundraiser for them, but a "friendraiser" for the whale.[3] They state that what inspired them to make the film is how many people were moved to share the whale's story, post about it, make work about it, in an effort to "connect." Ok, cupid, but connect to what, exactly? This whale? Whales in general? Other human enthusiasts of this phenomenon? People in general? Oneself?

However we answer this question, the crowdsourcing of the film *52: The Search for the Loneliest Whale in the World* speaks volumes about the contemporary connection starvation. If humpback songs were the soundtrack to imagining whale extinction and environmental death, this blue whale song is the soundtrack to another kind of death scene: the attrition of the social, particularly of love, sex, intimacy, friendship, connection, the more libidinal effects of what might be called "being heard" by another.

The idea of loneliness in connection with human-whale contact didn't begin with 52's plaintive signal. In 1961, anthropologist and nature writer Loren Eiseley wrote "The Long Loneliness," sometimes subtitled "Man and Porpoise, Two Solitary Destinies," in which he described humans as the loneliest beings in the universe because they deeply wish to but can't communicate with other animals. For Eiseley, the discovery that dolphins and porpoises may be another intelligence simply exacerbates the loneliness, as we realize how far away we are evolutionarily from cetaceans and how impossible it might be to ever come to understand them, despite their great intelligence. In rich, melancholy tones, Eisley ponders two sister lonelinesses, traveling through the world side by side and yet utterly unable to relieve each other's need to communicate:

It is difficult for us to visualize another kind of lonely, almost disembodied intelligence floating in the wavering green fairlyland of the sea—an intelligence possibly near or comparable to our own but without hands to build, to transmit knowledge by writing, or to alter by one hairsbreadth the planet's surface. . . . Without the stimulus provided by agile exploring fingers, these great sea mammals have yet taken a divergent road toward intelligence of a higher order. . . . It is as though both man and porpoise were each part of some great eye which yearned to look both outward on eternity and inward to the sea's heart—that fertile entity so like the mind in its swarming and grotesque life.[4]

Here, and in the rest of his writing, Eiseley has his finger on what Sagan later called our "cosmic loneliness," and to which he ascribed human motivation for the Voyager program, "our wish to end our isolation" and finally make contact with another intelligence.[5] But for Eiseley, cetaceans were just as lonely as humans, and while the human looked outward and became a philosopher, the porpoise was destined to wander "homeless across currents and winds and oceans, intelligent, but forever the lonely and curious observer of unknown wreckage falling through the blue light of eternity"[6]—a different kind of cosmic loneliness for a creature whose cosmos looks different.

Lonely and curious, human and whale: Eiseley's sensitive rendering of the porpoise who finds him- or herself just as "thrown" into the world as we are, who marvels at the mystery of creation and despairs at the limitations of embodied life, indicates how highly he esteemed cetacean intelligence and what he imagined to be their specific ways of being.

Is the loneliness for which 52 serves as the poster child still a cosmic loneliness, due to the gulfs between us and other intelligences, whether animal or alien? Cetaceans are once again enjoying a cultural moment, but the loneliness being thematized in our times seems specific to *humans as individuals, isolated from one another.* At the same time that we know more about whales than ever, we also find ourselves grasping at the remnants of models of social life that are quickly becoming extinct. In these conditions of social impoverishment, we turn to fantastic new visuals and re-turn to haunting audio recordings of the other most intelligent mammal, the sapiens of the sea. What kinds of projections are taking place as we find ourselves irresistibly drawn to these other vocalizing creatures, the most charismatic of the megafauna?

Our faith in cetacean intelligence is grounded in large part in the fact that they are acutely hearing creatures. The discovery that *Pakicetus*, the semi-aquatic wolf-like prehistoric mammal found in Pakistan in 1981, was a 50-million-year-old precursor to modern cetaceans, the "missing link" in whale evolution, was made thanks to the one piece of his skeleton that is found in whales today, the bone of the inner ear. The same is true of Basilosaurus, the enormous water creature whose remains were dug up in the 1830s in the United States, and who was finally classified as a whale on the basis of the inner ear bone, just a few years before Darwin published *On the Origin of Species*.[7]

Today, we know that dolphins have a capacity to hear and classify sounds in noisy environments that is unrivaled by any human-made listening device, and that dolphin biosonar, or their echolocation system, is also yet to be matched by any machine.[8] The only reason we do not have such data about larger odontocetes, like sperm whales, or any of the mysticetes, is because they're too big to be subjected to hearing tests in captivity.

But whales not only hear; they vocalize. Perhaps no other animal sound on the planet has a comparably powerful effect on the contemporary environmental imagination. How whale song affects us is the source of our belief that whales, like humans, are conversational creatures, with adjectives like "garrulous," "inquisitive," and "loquacious" popping up all over the scientific literature with no one blinking an eye or screaming "anthropomorphism!"[9]

There are complex projections at work in how we imagine the cetacean sounds themselves, or the specific fantasies about communication and relationships that cetaceans inspire. Dolphins and beluga whales are used in the heavily criticized practice of Dolphin Assisted Therapy for developmentally challenged children, whose proponents make various claims about the effects of whale sounds on human brains and bodies. Some claim that the sounds the animals make when they echolocate affect human tissue directly and promote healing of the body; others, that contact with these gentle and allegedly unconditionally loving creatures stimulates speech capacities in children with autism and Down syndrome.[10] Such thinking goes back to the sixties, when cetacean researchers suggested that cetaceans might have powers beyond what we can readily observe.

By 1970, physician John Sutphen had proposed using cetacean sounds in medical diagnosis, for example. He imagined echolocation as a form of x-ray vision that could see through skin and tissue. To cetaceans, "cancers and tumors must be self-evident. Strokes and heart attacks are as obvious as moles on our skins."[11] The move to use this for diagnosis in humans was adapted from earlier speculations about how dolphins echolocate problems inside each other's bodies, such as mothers noting the presence of gas in the stomachs of their babies (a potentially hazardous situation because it interferes with buoyancy), and burping them.[12] But Sutphen turns this into a speculation about *social* transparency among intelligent beings with echolocation, a point he calls "equally important and perhaps more interesting." "The psychophysiological alterations of sexual arousal, fear, depression, and excitement may be impossible to hide. . . . What sort of candor might exist between individuals where feelings are instantly or constantly bared?"[13]

The 1960s zeitgeist around cetaceans was ripe for such wild speculations. As Mette Bryld and Nina Lykke point out in their book, *Cosmodolphins*, in those days the dolphin typically functioned as a sort of spiritual doppelgänger, or what they describe as a new "noble savage" figure, "bearers of alternative values such as collectivity, compassion, friendliness, creativity, joyful sexuality, androgyny, spiritual wisdom and intuitive intelligence. . . ." Due in part to its capacity for communication, we imagined that "the whale [would] allegedly guide us to insight into the 'true and sacred' pleasures of a simple life in harmony with the natural environment" and each other. The interest in cetaceans was a direct response to the unlivability of modern life, serving as "the nostalgic imaginary of postindustrial culture, longing for an alternative world where the wounds inflicted by the destructive logic of present-day social relations between humans, technoscience and nature are healed; a world in which humans no longer seek to profit from the technoscientific control and domestication of nature."[14]

The writings of John C. Lilly, a psychoanalyst and neuroscientist who pushed the possibility of two-way communication further than anyone has, paints a picture of dolphin society as authentic, honest, and fundamentally good. He preceded Sutphen's fantasy of what John Durham Peters calls "dolphin sociability as applied radiology."[15] But where Sutphen associated echolocation itself with candor, due to its capacity to ferret out "the truth," it was Lilly who first imagined dolphins as a *speaking* species that does not use language to deceive.

Enthusiast of dolphin communication, isolation tanks, extraterrestrial life, and psychedelic drugs—often in combination—Lilly employed controversial techniques, from experiments in which he administered LSD to both himself and dolphins, to the now-famous story of his young assistant Margaret Howe Lovatt and her dolphin companion Peter, an extended communication-experiment-turned-interspecies "romance." But from such apparently nefarious activities emerged the possibility of alternatives to the horrors of modern human existence. Lovatt, who lived full time with Peter for two-and-a-half months, teaching him to mimic human sounds in English, wrote in her lab report, "I am implying the possibility of a lack of wheeling and dealing, of cheating and stealing and lying and other seemingly small but nevertheless devious ways of life stemming from human foible. From what I have observed and felt I do not feel that a dolphin newspaper, if one could exist, would contain articles on robbery, murder, dishonesty, delinquency, riots."[16]

John Durham Peters's recent book *The Marvelous Clouds* unwittingly takes up Lovatt's provocation about a dolphin newspaper and adapts it for today's media needs: "If they built an oceanwide web, it would have no archive but their collective brains and no search engines but their sonar." Peters is fascinated by the fact that dolphins have society in the absence of physical infrastructure, which he takes as a sign that their social bonds are simply stronger, truer than ours, and that this is because of how well they hear each other. "Humans learned to build ships, track stars, and write programs; and perhaps dolphins, having nothing better to do with their large brains, learned to pluck single voices out of the pitchy tangle of high-frequency noise."[17]

52 Blue strikes the imagination as such a tragic case precisely because the intelligence claim is inextricable from the claim about complex social life, and both are tied to the belief that such creatures must not only talk among themselves, but talk exceptionally *well*. Today, we have good reasons to continue to believe this about whale society, which is so tightly knit that they are willing (if that's the right word) to die together, as when entire groups get stranded at once, which is usually fatal. The leading explanation for this is that they are simply following an individual of their group that has gotten lost or sick and requires assistance.

Acoustic intelligence thus ends up becoming a sort of exceptional *social* intelligence. And one can't help but hear a faint longing in all of this work spanning the last sixty years, from Lilly to the Peters, for a social intelligence among humans that seems to be in short supply. We continue to simultaneously imagine and produce human collectivity over and against that of the other most loquacious, emotionally complex, and social animals on Earth. And when the newest, hottest online dating app, Happn, allows people to initiate a text exchange with someone they have actually crossed paths with in "real life"—thus operating entirely on the assumption that they won't have a real life chat without the app's help—it's no surprise that we hear 52 Blue's still unanswered transmission as a mating call.

3 LANGUAGE

Underlying all of these fantasies is the question of language, which remains unanswered in the case of cetaceans. That whales communicate is considered common knowledge. Bioacoustics has uncovered the richness and complexity of cetacean sounds and illuminated their central role in cetacean social organization. But the road is long from the type of communication that Vilém Flusser calls "natural," the conveying of information necessary for survival—whether aural like bird song or gestural like the waggle dance of bees—to what we call *language*. In contrast to natural communication, Flusser writes, the unnatural or "cultural" communication of humans is "perverse, because it wants to store the information it acquires."[1] Where does cetacean communication fall between these two possibilities? Scientists don't yet have an answer.

Analysis of humpback whale recordings took us pretty far toward thinking that whales might have language, when it was discovered that humpback pods seem to be communicating in idiolects, unique sound patterns that do not get repeated. The whales in one pod sing the same song, which changes over time in pitch and sometimes volume. Whales in the same area tend to sing the same song, but humpbacks elsewhere sing completely different songs, and patterns are not revisited over time, as one nineteen-year-long study has shown.[2] In other words, the particular songs on *Songs of the Humpback Whale* never appeared again, and probably never will. It seems as if humpbacks have discrete, shared songs that evolve over time, just like human language does.

Unlike humpbacks—who live in loosely knit, transient groups—orcas live in very stable pods, each of which has a discrete dialect. Although pods associate frequently, individuals never change pods and dialects are strictly maintained. In other words, there is no one "language" that could be called "orca," in a way similar to how there is no language that is called "human," while behavior and social organization indicates that linguistic communication is taking place within particular groups. Sperm whales are now thought to exhibit similar diversity among dialects to orcas. As with orcas, we still understand very little about how this works, but dialect is so central to sperm whale social life that scientists refer to the sperm whale social unit as a "vocal clan," a group that can number in the thousands of individuals.

Of all these species, it's the bottlenose dolphin that has historically inspired humans to attempt interspecies communication proper. Small, fast, agile, "chatty," promiscuous, energetic, playful, with brains roughly the same size as ours and seemingly very interested in us, dolphins provide the makings of irresistible experiments that might help us answer the question of cetacean language once and for all. Peters nails it when he writes that bottlenose dolphins are the species that "Marine Studios, *Flipper*, Sea World, the Cold War, and naval bioscience have made the royal road to cetacean knowledge."[3]

And yet Lilly, who devoted his life to experiments with odontocetes, did not posit that they have language. Good scientific practice demanded that he could not "accept the provisional working hypothesis of a whale language as anything more than a temporary aid to research design."[4] He did'nt need to show that whales have language, or even assume it, in order to attempt two-way communication. Much more pressing to Lilly was the idea of whale intelligence and their own interest in the communication experiments.

In 1965, Lovatt proposed to live with dolphins in a beautiful, sprawling home-turned-dolphinarium, which had been adapted into a laboratory of sorts and flooded with knee-deep water throughout. At the start of the live-in experiments, when Lovatt lived with Pamela the dolphin for a week, she concluded that the biggest factor in the rapid progress they were making toward two-way communication was "the dolphin's own interest and cooperation in seemingly just as strong an anxiety to 'get on with it.' We must remember that as they live and work with us they are learning not only the lessons in English and number systems, etc., they also are learning, just as we, about another way of life."[5] Their self-evident curiosity quickly became more important than any conclusive answer to the question of language.

Accordingly, Lilly and his team did not attempt to crack the code of dolphin sounds, since they were not sure that the sounds constituted a code. The most ambitious expression of the project was Lovatt living with Peter in Dolphin House for two-and-a-half months, as both worked daily at a getting Peter to "speak English," or rather to approximate human sounds instead of his squeaks, whistles, and clicks. The project took place on the island of St. Thomas and was funded by NASA.

From Lovatt's notes, it's clear that what was most remarkable about the experience of living with first Pamela and then Peter was just how far-reaching and complex the modes of relation became between human and dolphin under these bizarre conditions. She finds their daily encounters endlessly fascinating, while the world of people simultaneously bores her. For instance, she describes a situation in which people from the outside world, "all dry," came to see the laboratory and interacted with Peter by "leaning in" while he sprayed water at them from the flooded living room. Lovatt reports resentfully, "It is boring, eventually annoying, and completely out of line with what I am trying to do by living with Peter." She then seems to forget that Peter is actually in captivity, as if the depth of their relationship rendered them equally free agents: "Peter is not in a cage and will not be played with, teased, observed, stared at, or anything else by 'outside' people. You are several months too late, people, Peter has outgrown you." Lilly then adds parenthetically in the margins "(And so has Margaret.)."[6]

Today's two-way communication experiments are conducted with dolphins in the wild, indicating an even more powerful belief that they are interested in us and participate of their free will. Marine biologist Denise Herzing is currently attempting to communicate with a group of bottlenose dolphins in the Bahamas. She has teamed up with engineer Thad Starner to create the CHAT box, which records actual dolphin whistles and then plays them underwater in the proximity of objects. The hope is to create in the dolphin a referential, sound-for-object association by means of repetition, in the same way one teaches a child to speak.

This is the next step in research which has been going on for a while, in which scientists play dolphins' signature self-identifying whistles back to them underwater, to which the dolphins usually respond by whistling the same signature back. The CHAT device broadcasts not naming whistles, but discrete sounds, which Herzing wants her dolphins to associate with different, common objects. At present, the box broadcasts three sounds, for three objects: a scarf, a rope, and a piece of sargassum, a type of seaweed these dolphins often use as a toy. Herzing and Starner hope at some point to have a CHAT box with all the fundamental units of dolphin sound in it.

"In this sort of work it is wise to minimize the gadgetry and to maximize the use of one's self," wrote Lilly.[7]

Arguably, of course, gadgetry becomes necessary when dealing with such a dramatic difference as the one between air and water. But there is something about the underlying logic of CHAT that would have given Lilly pause, beginning with the gadgetry, but ending with a more abstract loss of what he must mean by "the use of one's self." What Herzing and Starner are most excited about in their work is the possibility of cracking the dolphin code by means of pattern recognition software, an algorithm that identifies order in what sounds to the human ear like a cacophony.[8] CHAT is essentially a context-aware smart device[9] focused on dolphin sounds and behaviors.

In other words, unlike Lilly, Herzing and Starner posit a dolphin language, and make communication contingent on decoding it by means of software. It is exactly this specific sense of "gadgetry" that Lilly worked hard to avoid, creating the most intimate, protracted contact possible by making the parties live together and letting communication be whatever arises between them under these conditions, rather than reducing it to the question of decipherment.

Lilly compared Margaret Lovatt to Jane Goodall because both women ended their experiments by marrying the photographers assigned to the job. Today, *National Geographic* calls Herzing "a veritable Jane Goodall of the sea," for reasons that have more to do with research methods than with her love life. In the end, it is still not the best comparison. While Goodall's ethological research on chimps in the wild indeed revolutionized primatology, it is not her work but the Great Ape Sign Language experiments of the 1970s that Herzing's dolphin research recalls. Although the project is aurally based, Herzing herself falls back into the sign language paradigm when discussing the process of dolphins learning CHAT: "Once they get it—like Helen Keller getting language—we think it's going to go very rapidly."[10] The slip is interesting: just as teaching chimps and gorillas to sign turned the focus away from both human and ape voices to sign language, our present attempts to communicate with dolphins have also led to a non-vocal technology.

Turning toward chimps and gorillas, we became an exaggeration of the creature we already were—a creature with hands. Turning toward dolphins, we have become an exaggeration of a different kind of creature, a creature with an underwater smart device. Whether or not being attached to a smart device is our new "natural" state, morphologically speaking, is a separate question. For now, it's enough to note that Thad Starner happens to also be the creator of Google Glass, the first attempt at pervasive computing that integrates seamlessly into the human body and never requires removing. In other words, with its pattern recognition software, the CHAT box is not just any gadget.

The backgrounding of the voice is significant, given that Lilly's work was grounded entirely in the vocalizing capacities dolphins and humans share, demanding of the dolphins that they learn to make humanoid sounds. With apes, the switch from voice to hands was to be expected, since apes in the wild use gestural communication with each other at least as much as vocalizing. Dolphins, however, are morphologically more distant from us, evolutionarily related to hoofed animals like deer and cattle, the hippo being their closest land relative. Ears seem to have replaced hands as their most prehensile organ, so to speak.

We abandoned the work with apes when they failed to use the signs they learned creatively and spontaneously, like human children do. We did not suspect apes of conversing with each other, and yet we never questioned the assumption that they would converse with us. Unfortunately for the experimental ape subjects, they "got it," but precisely *not* like Helen Keller, who (at least according to the famous and possibly apocryphal "getting it" scene in *The Miracle Worker*) became irrepressibly curious as soon as she understood that everything has a corresponding sign. Several of the sign language experiments, like Washoe the chimp and Koko the gorilla, were considered successful, but the entire enterprise was ultimately discredited in the course of the case of the chimpanzee Nim Chimpsky, whose keeper and observer Herbert Terrace concluded that apes were merely mimicking signs in order to please their trainers, not using them in the way that could count as language.

Even in the most successful cases, the apes failed to ask questions. Terrace stated that his motivation behind teaching Nim to sign was to "find out what the world looks like from a chimpanzee's point of view," but Nim never seemed invested in this project. The problem was a lack of curiosity, and eventually this spread to all parties involved, or, as Franz de Waal puts it, "Terrace found Nim a boring conversationalist."[11] The funding was pulled, the subjects were relocated, and the sun set on interspecies communication.

Today's project of communication with dolphins is a bit less ambitious in its goals, but it does bank on the well-documented curiosity of cetaceans, whose alleged innate interest in humans has fueled the whale watching and swimming-with-dolphins industries. Laws like the Marine Mammal Protection Act, Endangered Species Act, and Fisheries Act restrict how closely humans and vessels may approach cetaceans, but not vice versa. This means that the only way to get close to a gray whale or swim with a dusky dolphin in open water is if the creature freely approaches you or your vessel.

This happens often in the case of gray whales, dusky dolphins, and belugas, all famously curious species, but has also been documented in orcas. In the case of the orca named Luna, his powerful desire for interaction with humans is the centerpiece of the 2011 documentary *The Whale* (dir. Chisholm and Parfit, 2012). Luna was a juvenile, separated from his pod and living alone in Nootka Sound, where he consistently and aggressively sought out the company and touch of humans, to the point where whale conservationists began working hard to restrict the contact, ostensibly for Luna's safety. At first, the story seems focused on Luna's desire for contact as proof of his personhood. But there's an underlying narrative, that of human interestingness to non-humans smart enough to notice. Many of the film's speakers comment throughout on how extraordinary it is that a *wild* animal, free to swim away at every moment, would be this interested in "us."

Likewise, the fact that the CHAT experiments are conducted in the wild assumes a certain level of human attractiveness, to which other intelligences will just naturally be drawn. It is remarkable, then, that in the CHAT universe, meaning is reduced to direct correspondence between sounds and the things to which they symbolically refer, in other words, to the part of speech that is *least* likely to inspire interest. The dolphins are asked to enter into an agreement with the gadget-wielding human that this whistle in fact means "scarf," this other one in fact means "sargassum," and that one, "rope." If cetacean social life is as heavily lubricated by conversation as Herzing and Starner imagine, if theirs is a subjectivity unusually ravenous for novel and complex stimuli and an intersubjectivity as authentically inter-attuned as Lilly and Lovatt suggest, why would this mundane, superficial, utterly contrived interaction catch and hold their interest? Why should they care?

4 INTEREST

As a strictly empirical claim, the working hypothesis that cetaceans might find us mind-numbingly boring sounds like something out of *The Hitchhiker's Guide to the Galaxy*. To be clear, I don't propose to know what they feel or think about humans or anything else.[1] What interests me is, first of all, the value that we place on curiosity in the research, second, how much we treat that same highly valued cetacean curiosity as a constant that we can take entirely for granted, and third, that we are doing so in a world in which curiosity seems to be in ever-shorter supply.

In his Object Lessons book *Silence* John Biguenet identifies the connection between noise, technology, and our instruments of knowledge. He writes that the value of silence is soaring in a clamorous world, made more clamorous by the technologies we devise in order to know it better, hoping, ironically, to shut down all that clamor once and for all by coming to know everything there is to know. Along with silence the ineffable "continues to contract."[2]

Loren Eiseley's meditations on knowledge acquisition as a form of listening invite similar comparisons:

Man, too, lies at the heart of a web, a web extending through the starry reaches of sidereal space, as well as backward into the dark realm of prehistory. His great eye upon Mount Palomar looks into a distance of millions of light years, his radio ear hears the whisper of even more remote galaxies, he peers through the electron microscope upon the minute particles of his own being. It is a web no creature of earth has ever spun before. Like the orb spider, man lies at the heart of it, listening.[3]

Eiseley is often caught between his deep sense of wonder at human accomplishment on one hand and his powerful conviction that we are animals one the other, and he struggles to reconcile these into a unified account of earthly existence. But the image of the thinking creature as one who waits and listens—whether human, squirrel, bird, or spider—is consistent throughout his work. It's not that one listens to or for silence, it's that silence is the condition of every listening. It must be there in order for listening to happen at all. The ineffable is that thing about which we are, precisely, inexhaustibly curious, that for which we listen.

In a sense, then, we are curious about that which we are *not* smart about, and often, that which we suspect may continue to exceed the grasp of our knowledge. If intelligence and curiosity are related, so are intelligence and boredom, or a disappointed curiosity. The intelligent creature is one whose interest will not be captured by just anything. Hence my question: why should dolphins be interested in the poor excuse for a conversation that CHAT offers them?

CHAT departs so dramatically from the goals of Lilly and his team as to be incompatible with them. The group's director was none other than Gregory Bateson, husband of Margaret Mead and himself a celebrated anthropologist. He wrote up his observations of the operation in an extraordinary article about preverbal mammals from 1966. "We might say that the whale is the communicational opposite of the giraffe; it has no neck, but has a voice," he mused, going on to speculate about what this difference might mean for mammals that have evolved to communicate almost entirely without facial expressions, eye contact, or hands.[4]

The hands were especially key for him, because the cetacean world is not a world populated by things. This was the difference, or what Bateson liked to call "the difference that makes a difference," that distinguished cetaceans from humans and put them in the same category as other preverbal mammals, making theirs a communication specifically about relationships.

I personally do not believe that the dolphins have anything that a human linguist would call language. I do not think that any animal without hands would be stupid enough to arrive at so outlandish a mode of communication. To use a syntax and category system appropriate for the discussion of things that can be handled, while really discussing the patterns and contingencies of relationship, is fantastic. . . . Preverbal mammals communicate about things, when they must, by using what are primarily [relationship]-function signals. In contrast, human beings use language, which is primarily oriented toward things, to discuss relationships.[5]

Bateson thus might have rejected the CHAT approach completely on the grounds that it focuses on things.

Recent research questions the strong distinction he makes between the two types of communication, on the grounds that the worlds of some preverbal mammals are more populated by things than we initially thought. Some preverbal mammals do use "thing" language and have some form of rudimentary syntax. Vervet monkeys (another mammal with hands), for example, have distinct alarm calls for different predators, not just one call for "danger," because different sources of danger call for different behaviors. And in the end, in his usual fashion of wonder and humility before how much we do not know, Bateson allowed for the more open possibility that cetacean communication is actually not describable in these terms at all, but is in fact so different from that of terrestrial mammals, both human and not, that we can't imagine or empathize with it.[6] But whatever the details, he was certain that cetaceans talk more about relation than we do. From this perspective, the CHAT experiments would not be speaking their language, as it were, and the whole experiment is simply badly constructed.

If Bateson is right, this allows for the possibility of another kind of critique of CHAT, one based on ethological observations not of dolphins, but of humans. Why should cetaceans be drawn to creatures that are arguably becoming less and less good at relating? Why would they swim toward creatures holding smart devices when, in the human social world, the smart device acts as a social deterrent, as anyone knows who has sat at a bar and watched people interacting with their phones instead of each other? Like Lilly and Lovatt, Bateson liked to playfully speculate about dolphin social intelligence, musing that "the presence of all sort of courtesy rules in this business; it probably isn't polite to sonar scan your friends too much, just as among humans it is not polite, really, to look too closely at another's feet in detail."[7] Such sensitive creatures would require us to be more interesting than the constraints of CHAT allow.

While Bateson might have rejected the first stage of CHAT, namely the prerecorded whistles, it's the second stage, the pattern recognition software, that poses the biggest challenge to curiosity. The technology Starner uses to study dolphins is something he plans to apply to all human activity, in hopes of finally making every last aspect of life intelligible. He envisions software that "can discover the signature of any activity, from brushing your teeth to commuting to work," a wearable computer that can literally "decode" the most banal and idiosyncratic gestures and activities and map them out as learnable "language." In his words: "Imagine having sensors on your wrist, and as you go through daily life, it could figure out what paging through a book is, opening the car door. All these things are unique gestures," which become "scripts" when computers learn them.[8]

In other words, the cacophony Starner wishes to decode is the one of life itself. Google Glass has disappeared temporarily, but, as *MIT Technology Review* reports, we are only in the beginning stages of context-aware pervasive computing, which will become the center of our lives, serving as "a memory aid and productivity enhancer."[9] The goal of ubiquitous computing is life become script, completely, exhaustively predictable, learnable by computers in the form of phones, glasses, watches, vibrators, dust, and who knows what other smart thing will soon accompany everyday life.

Lilly urged human researchers to have faith in the working hypothesis that "both we and they are intelligent enough to break the interspecies communication barrier between these very different minds."[10] But intelligence is not the only thing at stake these days, and Lilly often conflates intelligence and interestingness, as when he writes, "The sperm whales have brains six times the size of ours. Before they are annihilated by man, I would like to exchange ideas with a sperm whale. I am not sure that they would be interested in communicating with me because my brain is obviously is much more limited than theirs."[11] And yet we humans, who assume that the brains of other mammals are more limited than ours, are still quite interested in communicating with them.

Thus, mine is not exactly the same question that de Waal poses in the title of his recent book, *Are We Smart Enough to*

Know How Smart Animals Are?, because the problem is not that we don't know enough, but that we know "too much," in exactly the same sense smart devices may be imagined as making us dumber.

Smart devices are an alarming symptom of the contraction of the ineffable in modern life. In a world in which, as Jean-François Lyotard puts it, "everything that is to be done is as if it were already done," what remains to be curious about?[12] In his essay "Interesting?" Lyotard announces that "nothing is less interesting" than what passes for conversation these days: "Bergson said, conversation is conservation. The same goes for the majority of interviews, discussions, dialogues, roundtables, debates, colloquia for which our world has such an appetite. They serve to assure that we are indeed 'on the same wavelength' and that it's going OK. Nothing is less interesting."[13] In *this* noisy century, there is certainly no lack of speech. But it's reasonable to assume that intelligent, interested creatures would not wish to talk to creatures that talk to each other without saying anything.

Recent work in critical animal studies is missing a crucial point: that even as we come to realize how interesting animals truly are—a claim easy to establish in the case of cetaceans—we ourselves are becoming less so. For example, Vinciane Despret's work on lab rats in "Thinking Like A Rat" explores how research changes when scientists factor in the idea that the rat has a perspective on the experiment. In other words, simply allowing for the possibility that the rat might be behaving not only in direct response to stimuli but under the rule of the question *what is expected of me?* has effects on the experiment's results. The question of perspective ends here for both the lab scientists and Despret, with the rat's perspective on the experiment. But what about its perspective on *us*?

And what about the further question of "our" (shared) perspective? The case of CHAT invites us to extend Despret's frame to ask whether we, the smart-device wielding humans, can still be described as creatures with perspective. After all, writing the complete script of life demands the leveling of different perspectives and unique gestures. Despret rightly writes, "Animals do not judge an abstract situation, but a situation is offered to them as it is offered to them."[14] But can we say the same thing about ourselves in the era of smart devices? As computing becomes ever more pervasive, is there still a "human perspective" from which other intelligent beings, for instance cetaceans, might hope to learn about the world?

Donna Haraway writes about Despret's unique take on relationships with experimental animals, that "it demands the ability to find others actively interesting, even or especially others most people already claim to know all too completely, *to ask questions that one's interlocutors truly find interesting*, to cultivate the wild virtue of curiosity. . . ."[15] But we might wonder whether to be interested and to be interesting can be strung together so automatically. Asking questions that one's interlocutors truly find interesting will be the difficult task, but absolutely essential if we wish to enter into such relations of authentic, reciprocal observation. The question, then, even for research concerned with animal intelligence, is not, are *we smart enough. . .?* or *are we interested enough. . .?*, but rather *are we interesting enough to ever find out how smart animals are?*

5 CHARISMA

A recent headline in the *Onion* reads "Dolphin Spends Amazing Vacation Swimming with Stockbroker:"

ORLANDO, FL—Describing the encounter as a once-in-a-lifetime experience she'll never forget, local bottlenose dolphin Hazel reportedly recounted stories Tuesday from a recent vacation in which she got to go swimming with a stockbroker. "He was definitely shy at first, but with a little encouragement he swam right up next to me—the whole thing was so amazing," said the dolphin, appearing excited as she described her "almost spiritual" encounter with the financial executive, whom she estimated was perhaps 40 years old and weighed as much as 180 pounds. "And he was just chattering away the whole time. It's like they have their own little language. You have to wonder what's going on in their heads and whether it's true that they're almost as intelligent as we are." The dolphin added that while she ultimately enjoyed her experience, she was disappointed that she wasn't allowed to actually ride the stockbroker.[1]

The joke hangs on the figure of the stockbroker, middle-aged, wealthy enough to afford this, with no other particularly interesting characteristics—the stereotype of the upwardly mobile human whose inner life is so impoverished that he must seek out experiences like swimming with dolphins in order to feel alive again.

Why do cetaceans fascinate so? The appeal of whales lives at the intersection of two attractions—to the sea and to what scientists call "charismatic megafauna." In *Wildlife in the Anthropocene*, geographer Jamie Lorimer argues that what was once denigrated as "anthropomorphism" is basically the same thing as what is now less problematically classified as "charisma," one of the "passions that power conservation." Lorimer considers charisma a more-than-human phenomenon, claiming that animals have "their own ways of perceiving and evaluating the charisma of those with whom they cohabit," including humans.[2]

Perhaps the most famous example of interspecies attractions among non-human animals is Koko the gorilla having a pet kitten. But this is old news; the Internet now brings us daily updates about interspecies relations in the wild, especially in life-threatening situations (lioness saves baby deer from other lions, orangutan saves baby bird from drowning), but not only (polar bear pets dog, cat loves dolphin). Humpbacks as a species are now thought to exhibit great altruism and empathy toward other species, whom they try to save from orca attacks. In a recent study of humpbacks intervening in orca attacks, 89 percent of those interventions took place when the orcas attacked species other than humpbacks.[3]

But as we discover more and more contexts in which animals of various species interact in emotionally complex ways that suggest altruism, affinity, empathy, and indeed charisma, Lorimer's analysis would benefit from a broader look at the loss of charisma among humans. It seems that certain species of fauna become more charismatic to us, the less charismatic we become to one another.

The case of Timothy Treadwell, the Grizzly Man made famous by Werner Herzog in the film by the same name, makes this point dramatically.[4] Treadwell hated people, but without any articulable reason. Like many of us, he was simply disappointed, but unlike many of us, he chose to live among bears rather than humans. The film contains consistent examples of his displaced desire, like a less-than-appropriate interest in bear feces (which he holds in his hand while exclaiming passionately, "This was inside her!") and focuses on Treadwell as a complicated, unstable, and lusty being, implying that the orgiastic end to which he came, torn to bits and eaten by a hungry bear, was exactly what he'd secretly wanted all along. When Herzog listens to the audio of the fatal bear attack over headphones, and quietly instructs Treadwell's open-mouthed ex-girlfriend to never, ever listen to it, it is almost as if they were discussing a sex tape she must never see.

But *Grizzly Man* is more than a decade old now. A more recent example is Thomas Thwaites's "GoatMan" work, in which he wore a prosthetic stomach and legs in order to live among goats in Switzerland. This time, the goal to get away from humans is both clearly articulated and absolutely undramatic. Thwaites is a sort of cultural theorist and humorist who received a grant for this work and wrote a book under the same title. He describes a deliberate attempt to get away from human social life and the proverbial "rat race," in order to come to understand the world from a completely different perspective. Describing himself in terms that resonate deeply for most twenty-first-century humans, he states, "I was fed up with my life anyway and I needed a break. I was jobless and I had a lot of personal problems, and I found everyday life so stressful."[5]

His turn toward animal life is also predictable, a feeling many of us have had on the heels of such frustrations: "One day I was walking with the dog of a friend and I noticed that the dog just seemed really happy about life, without any worries, and I thought to myself it would be really great to be you for a day."[6] His realization emerged from walking a friend's dog, not years of philosophizing or hermit-like misanthropy. After seriously contemplating becoming an elephant, he settled on the goat as his animal of choice and began the project of living among goats as one of the herd.

Thwaites's work is intelligent and hipster-funny, and the obviousness of its premises and conclusions contributes to Thwaites's "everyman" persona and ideas-industrial appeal. If we openly mock the stockbroker for swimming with dolphins in order to get in touch with his feelings, the laughter at GoatMan is of a different sort. In fact, GoatMan's great value lies in how it puts our ambivalence about it on display: *is* this a joke? We all immediately recognize ourselves in his low-grade depression, and his turn, however heavily technologically mediated, to an animal that can not only stand its own herd, but that even has the social generosity to welcome a lone outsider on all fours.

Most of us don't have the opportunity to try it out in real life. Instead, protracted stress and disappointment with our lives and relationships coincides with fantasy projections onto wild animals we see on screens: the Monterey Bay Aquarium's otter live cam, for instance, or Ocearch's Global Shark Tracker app that tracks the activity of wild sharks on smartphones in real time. And the concept of charisma is no longer sufficient to account for the pull of animals against the background of contemporary visual-digital culture.

Recent research into the phenomenon called "cute aggression" has shown that people looking at photos of cute animals were overwhelmed by a desire to squeeze those animals. Hard. "Some participants even experienced a loss of control – that is, a participant finds an animal is so cute that he or she 'can't handle it.'"[7] Psychologists attribute the aggression response to an excess of positive affect: the pleasure at seeing the baby panda or the sloth hugging the kitten is so acute that the viewer experiences a brief bout of insanity. We lose it. "Another possibility is that it's just too much of a good thing—sometimes we portray an onslaught of positive emotion in a negative way, like when you're so happy you cry. There is speculation that experiencing the positive affect negatively might help people 'regulate that high energy.'"[8]

But these conclusions miss some crucial points. First, this is a first world phenomenon. In their skit, "Cute Puppies," comedians Key and Peele play women on a mid-workday stroll who suddenly happen upon a puppy in a pet-shop window. The puppy's cuteness has affected them so powerfully that their mindless, gossipy, Valley-Girl-inflected chatter turns to increasingly intricate scenarios of cruelty and killing. Both African American (although one reads as more mixed-race than the other), the comedians owe their fame to skits satirizing blackness. In "Cute Puppies," however, the female characters are unmistakably white and middle class, in hairstyle, dress, and speech, but perhaps most importantly, thanks to that ubiquitous indicator of whiteness, expensive coffees to go (featured on stuffwhitepeoplelike.com). Key and Peele have their fingers on the new figure of the American Psycho. Ecstatic expressions of sadism toward cute animals are not some underlying truth of the human psyche, but very specific cracks in the armor of contemporary culture—upwardly mobile, emotionally repressed, inauthentic, superficial, competitive, and dissociative.

It's probably no accident that the Internet Cat Video Festival began in the belly of the beast of privileged America (hello, Brooklyn!) before it spread to other American cities and most recently to the UK. While everyone seems to agree that there's something weirdly hilarious about the fact that the first world sits at home watching cute animal videos, this most recent version of the animal obsession remains unexplored by scientists, except some evolutionary psychologists, who tie it all back to human investment in human babies, rather than investigating it as a relationship with animals in particular.

And yet, as of now, there has never been an Internet Baby Video Festival. And cute aggression is animal-specific in practice. While what is normally recognized as "cruelty to animals" is traditionally considered a symptom of social breakdown under conditions of great economic stress (think of staged dog fights in poor urban areas, for instance), people have invented a new, less obvious form of it for the first world. Animal cruelty is the fraying of the social fabric, humans at their weakest and most desperate, a screaming symptom of "deficiencies in the supportive quality of the social environment."[9] While no one would call cat videos "animal cruelty," given the intense affects these experiences elicit, the phrase seems appropriate. Is this new "frenzy of the visible" around animals in particular, a phrase I borrow from Linda Williams's work on pornography, tied to the attrition of social life?

After all, we're not just talking about photos of cats or babies. We're talking about "content" circulating on social media, a specific form of communication, one of the main options currently available to us. Consumers of this content are also consumers of the *form* of communication, with everything it enables and constrains. And no matter how aware we are of social media's manipulations, as Dominic Pettman writes, "we are still vulnerable to their solicitations and seductions. Why? Because we are creatures who, above all, need to communicate (*homo communis*). So when it comes to the consumers of the means of communication, affect trumps knowledge. This is why we may curse Zuckerberg's name yet continue to click around Facebook."[10]

When coming to understand our affective states around certain imagery, we should remember that we're simultaneously consumers of a means of communication, or of the circulation of that imagery. Having "quit" Facebook for the second time several years ago, I often find myself wondering if I should return. When I poll my friends, all of whom are on it, all of them, without exception, tell me it's terrible, depressing, and a waste of time, and urge me to stay away. And all of them, without exception, can't seem to deactivate their own pages.

In 2016, a baby Franciscana dolphin was pulled from shallow waters on an Argentinian beach and died while beachgoers passed it around and took selfies with it.[11] Whale and Dolphin Conservation, the leading global charity dedicated to cetacean conservation, published a blog post titled "We Should Stop Taking Selfies and Start Looking in the Mirror" following the well-publicized death. In this case, our connection-starvation translated so literally into taking selfies and presumably immediately posting them to social media that the actual encounter with the dolphin quickly became unsustainable. Death by Instagram. The public outrage about this event also took place on social media, where everything takes place, without the slightest suspicion that these new agencies, at once strange and utterly banal, motivated by the desire to connect, are contributing to environmental loss far beyond the death of this one dolphin.

The Franciscana or La Plata species is listed as vulnerable. In his work on extinction, Thom Van Dooren has coined the term "avian entanglements," which I will adapt here to discuss cetacean entanglements like the one above. "These are relationships of co-evolution and ecological dependency. But they are also about more than 'biology' in any narrow sense. It is inside these multispecies entanglements that learning and development take place, that social practices and cultures are formed."[12] The Fransciscana case is a striking example of cetacean entanglement. "Wild animals are not toys or photo props. They should be appreciated—and left alone—in the wild where they belong," stated a spokesperson for World Animal Protection.[13] But is a crowded beach "the wild"? And who belongs in this liminal space, at once marine and terrestrial?

And finally, of course, wild animals have been photo props for centuries, since wilderness became one of the most revered photographic subjects, in direct response to the emotional problems resulting from industrialization and development. Donna Haraway names such situations "permanent complexity."[14]

A less tolerant name may be found in what Lauren Berlant calls "slow death," which I will stretch here beyond its meaning for humans. Slow death is when life building and the attrition of life become indistinguishable processes, a situation in which the very things one must do in order to have a life are the things that lessen the quality of life. If Nietzsche's dictum in *Twilight of the Idols*, "that which does not kill us makes us stronger," was a sort of mantra for modernity, the present moment seems to announce something different. In the case of whales and humans, life-building processes like wilderness recreation contribute directly to animal and environmental death. As late moderns, we're coming to realize that that which does not kill us in fact slowly kills us.

6 CAPTIVITY

Blackfish (dir. Cowperthwaite), the 2013 documentary about Sea World, offers up another kind of cetacean entanglement, one grounded in an earlier form of the society of the spectacle than that of the selfie-snapping Argentines. Whale trainer Dawn Brancheau was not just killed, but also partly eaten by her beloved orca, Tilikum, immediately following a "Dine with Shamu" show. Though the cause of her death was drowning and blunt trauma to the head, several moments in the film imply that she was eaten, or something like it ("he still has her" and "his mouth had to be pried open"). That Tilikum ate Bracheau is not just a detail among others. Since humans are not a natural part of any orca diet (no hominid is a natural part of any marine mammal diet), the event of Brancheau's death reeks of a sort of perversion of nature. He ate her precisely because he had been removed from his proper place in the world, and lived his entire life in the human-made ecosystems of first Sealand and later Sea World.

The film is a document of contemporary social toxicity and the impact of captivity on intelligent animals. And yet by the end, one cannot help but feel that humans, too, are suffering from what can only be described as captivity. *Blackfish* shows a multi faceted perversity of consumption—visual, economic, and bodily—in which the audience consumes the Shamu spectacle at the same time as Tillikum literally consumes Bracheau.

This is not as exotic as it may at first seem. Cetacean entanglements are shaped by consumption on many levels, not the least of which is the fact that despite the International Whaling Commission's (IWC) 1982 ban on commercial whaling, Japan, Norway, and Iceland continue to hunt whales for the purposes of eating them. Japan claims to hunt whales for research, but sells whale meat as food. Norway and Iceland both overtly reject the moratorium and serve whale meat mainly to tourists, so that they may have an "authentic" local experience.

As we turn to tourism as a form of relief from the pressures of modern life, looking to authentic experiences to provide meaning and depth to our difficult lives, something like the promise of "the real Iceland" is naturally seductive. The whale hunt takes place right next to the whale watching area in Reykjavik, a bizarre fact that the International Fund for Animal Welfare uses, in turn, in the catchy title of its anti-whaling campaign, "Meet Us, Don't Eat Us."[1] But whale watching is itself a form of consumption grounded in the same mechanics of spectacle at work in Sea World shows, the mechanics of relief or escape from daily life experienced as a form of captivity.

Blackfish is an argument for the personhood of orcas, but this personhood is demonstrated not by the usual means (signs of intellectual complexity, capacity for communication, elaborate social structures), but by Tilikum's aggression, presented as something like a revolutionary act of violence: anti-colonial, proletarian—or both. Tilly's murderous, perverted despair is our own. It is not Brancheau but Tilly who is presented as the new figure of consuming in captivity, trapped not only in his tank but in the socio-ecologically toxic environment we quickly come to recognize as the same one in which we are trapped.

Blackfish, the biggest film about whales since *Free Willy*, ends with black dorsal fins deftly cutting the glimmering waters of the Pacific Northwest, as the former Sea World trainers tear up at the sight of orcas swimming in pods in the wild, open waters, in sharp contrast to Sea World's despairing captives. And the emotional power of the end of the film is about more than orca freedom; after witnessing how violent, corrupt, exploitative, deluded, and cruel humans are to animals and each other, anyone would like to jump in the water and swim away, far away from here. Wilderness is presented as the other side of captivity, as the freedom of expansive spaces, solitude, authenticity, and unmediated, natural relations.

But is the ocean a wilderness? Unlike terrestrial wilderness, oceans were never human habitats, so in some ways, oceanscapes answer our desires for the wild literally and unproblematically. The ocean is the ultimate wide-open space. But while humans never lived in the sea, their very distant ancestors certainly did, as did those of all land animals. This complicates how we imagine the ocean as habitat. Eiseley captures some of this ambivalence: "Every time we walk along a beach some ancient urge disturbs us so that we find ourselves shedding shoes and garments or scavenging among seaweed and whitened timbers like the homesick refugees of a long war."[2]

Rachel Carson peppered *The Sea Around Us* with reminders that the sea is the humans' ancestral home. She identified our modern, technologically mediated fascination with sea life as a moment in the evolutionary arc that ties humans to their ancient marine beginnings: "Eventually, man, too, found his way back to the sea. . . . Moving in fascination over the deep sea he could not enter, he found ways to probe its depths, he let down nets to capture its life, he invented mechanical eyes and ears that could re-create for his senses a world long lost, but a world that, in the deepest part of his subconscious mind, he had never wholly forgotten."[3]

The adoption of the nautical metaphor for space exploration uses the same trope of return to origins. As the environmental movement grew in popularity, Carl Sagan's *Cosmos* series depicted the blackness of space as an ocean and planets as worlds. The medium in which the worlds were suspended was simply . . . nothing. In his book by the same title, Sagan writes poetically: "The surface of the Earth is the shore of the cosmic ocean. From it we have learned most of what we know. Recently, we have waded a little out to sea, enough to dampen our toes or, at most, wet our ankles. The water seems inviting. The ocean calls. Some part of our being knows this is from where we came. We long to return."[4] And yet, just beyond the beaches on which we dampen our toes, the open sea continues to exceed environmental imagination altogether. Long considered empty space, as Stacy Alaimo writes, "beyond state borders, legal protection, and cultural imaginaries," the open sea is as far away as possible from the classic terrestrial stewardship logic of modern environmentalism.[5]

The ocean makes up a whopping 99 percent of the biosphere. Fourth-fifths of all biomass exists in the ocean. However, the passions that animate traditional environmentalism are grounded entirely in a commitment to "the land." Likewise, as soon as we head out further into the inviting "waters" of Sagan's space its vastness and darkness become overwhelming. "The Earth is a place. It is by no means the only place. It is not even a typical place. No planet or galaxy can be typical, because the cosmos is mostly empty. The only typical place is within the vast, cold, universal vacuum, the everlasting night of intergalactic space, a place so strange and desolate that, by comparison, planets and stars and galaxies seem achingly rare and lovely . . . . Worlds are precious."[6] The space/water itself, it seems, is much less so.

This may be one reason we never seem to worry that our debris in space might someday become a problem, just as we thought until recently that the ocean was a bottomless dumping ground here on Earth. But it turns out that even space debris is becoming dangerous. A 2011 report by the US National Research Council warned NASA that orbiting space debris was at a critical level, at which collisions with spacecraft were imminent, which in turn creates more space debris.[7]

Our inability to think non-terrestrially is necessarily accompanied by other constraints on environmental imagination, as this passage from Scott Russell Sanders's *A Conservationist Manifesto* illustrates:

> It should go without saying that we encounter real places not by gazing through windshields or by gaping at screens but by walking. Alluring places invite us to immerse ourselves, to open all our senses . . . . By comparison, the world presented by the electronic media is disembodied, stripped down, anemic, and hasty. The more time we spend in the virtual world, the more likely we are to forget how impoverished it is . . . . The actual world, the three dimensional array of sights and textures and tastes and sounds that we find in a vibrant city or landscape, needs no hype in order to intrigue us.[8]

Against the received view of what counts as a place (where walking is possible and all senses can be "open") and what counts as robust, sensuous perception of a place worth protecting, the ocean faces many challenges.[9] On screen, it becomes two-dimensional. Its abyssal, murky vastness does not map easily onto the conservationist model of "a geography of somewhere, . . . worthy of a visitor's deep engagement and of a citizen's love."[10]

Google Earth's recent attempt at addressing this raises problems of its own. As it continues to grow and offer ever more unprecedented, interactive cartographical delights, inviting us since 2011 to explore large swaths of the seafloor using our devices, all that Google Earth can see, and all that its demo videos present as worthy of exploring, is the sea*floor*, its terrestrial part. The sea as other-than-terrestrial remains beyond Google's panoptical scope.

So how can we come to love the sea? Just as Watlington was recording his humpbacks, Jacques Cousteau and Louis Malle released their 1956 documentary *The Silent World*, one of the first films to use underwater cinematography to show the ocean in color. "People protect what they love" was Cousteau's famous dictum, launching his career as the person who brought the wonders of the deep sea into America's living rooms with his hit TV show *The Undersea World of Jacques Cousteau*, a documentary series that ran for a full decade from 1966 to 1976. Today, most of us continue to "access" the open ocean and the deep sea only by gaping at screens—but this is no longer the golden age of television. The contemporary experience of the screen is different than in Cousteau's heyday, and the social imaginary in which contemporary visual culture thrives brings with it different challenges and constraints than those of the television era.

It could be argued that it is not just geographical wilderness, but wild animals themselves that offer the promise of escape from captivity. For Lilly and Lovatt, living with dolphins was in many ways preferable to living among humans. Reading Lilly's meditations on humanity, in which he advises "all extraterrestrial visitors to avoid man. He is a dangerous, unpredictable, powerful, 'bright animal', operating in murderous concert," one gets the feeling that contact with intelligent non-humans provides the only possible escape from corrupt and toxic earthly social life.[11]

An earlier example of this kind of thinking is *Ring of Bright Water* (1960), Gavin Maxwell's extraordinary journal of isolation and his love for his pet otters in a remote village in western Scotland, where he describes life with otters as freedom from the "prison" of modern life and social relations.[12] It should come as no surprise that both Lilly and Maxwell had social class on their side, and the resources to escape to remote locations and raise marine mammals as companions (or keep them as pets, depending on whom you ask).

Economics is never *not* at work here, which is why the *Onion*'s imaginary dolphin-lover is a stockbroker. The very real scene in which a baby dolphin dies in the hands of the Argentinian beachgoers suggests a contrast that just underscores the fantasy: the unthinking, undifferentiated, orgiastically selfie-snapping mass, the common people who because of sheer numbers and lack of subtlety and education destroy everything they touch, even, or especially, when treasures are offered to them. On the other side of the promise of wilderness is the ominous rumble of mass society. Always. For this reason, as I have written about elsewhere, understanding mass media is indispensable to any progressive environmental thinking.[13]

Perhaps nowhere is this truer than in the case of the sea and its inhabitants. Unlike Lilly and Maxwell, today most of us experience cetaceans primarily on screen. Jamie Lorimer points to what he calls "the logic of awe" in which megafauna are often depicted in films, an effect that contributes to the illusion of massive distance between their habitats and ours. But this is especially pronounced in the case of cetaceans, who are at once so close to us in terms of intelligence, and so far from us in terms of anatomy and habitat. Their alienness is constantly underscored by the visual narratives in which we encounter them. "Great attention is given to portraying their alien ecologies, unfamiliar anatomies, and inhuman behaviors," linking the logic of awe to the romantic tradition of the sublime and "in popular incarnations—especially those targeted at North American audiences—the sublime elides with the cult of wilderness and an apocalyptic understanding of environmental change."[14]

Lorimer questions the idea that such romantic, awesome imagery fosters respect for difference, calling it almost pornographic, as "we are presented with an improbable feast of expansive and unpopulated locations inhabited by exotic animals, which are forever fighting, fucking, eating, migrating, and dying for their impatient channel-surfing audiences."[15] Indeed, images of whales are high on the list of awesome wildlife imagery, from recent big budget undertakings like BBC's *Ocean Giants* to DareWin's virtual reality content. As Bryld and Lykke argue in *Cosmodolphins*, "The simultaneous act of cannibalizing and worshipping the wild . . . is being replayed today."[16]

The logic of awe, and thus the contemporary presentation of wild animals, is subject to what environmental historian William Cronon has named "the trouble with wilderness" in his essay by that title, in which he criticized the idea of wilderness as a form of something like false consciousness. We can live out our not-so-wild lives better just knowing that an alternative exists out there, beyond the threshold of mundane terrestrial life:

> We inhabit civilization while holding some part of ourselves—what we imagine to be the most precious part—aloof from its entanglements. By imagining that our true home is in the wilderness, we forgive ourselves the homes we actually inhabit. In its flight from history, in its siren song of escape, in its reproduction of the dangerous dualism that sets human beings outside of nature—in all of these ways, wilderness poses a serious threat to responsible environmentalism at the end of the twentieth century.[17]

This dualism gets reproduced again in our imagining of what Bryld and Lykke call the "extraterrestrial commons," the cosmos and the ocean, both of which offer an escape from once-wild, now-ruined Earth.

The more rapidly our "civilized" ways of living devour the wild, the more we middle-class people of postindustrial cultures become obsessed with a radical nostalgia for healing the broken bonds between human and wild nature. Vanishing terrestrial wildernesses are reinvented in the shape of "wilderness parks," or reconstructed as "virtual reality" images, and new extraterrestrial ones, the cosmos and the ocean, brought into focus.[18]

Might the recent popular turn to ocean conservation be just another form of escape, a new layer of the trouble?

While most terrestrial wilderness is de-historicized when we willfully forget human habitation (in the case of Native American removal, most notably), marine wilderness is de-historicized when we willfully forget human impact. Alaimo writes that the disconnection between terrestrial humans and "the vast liquid habitats that cover much of the planet" makes it easier to distance ourselves from what is in fact an enormous human presence inside oceans in the following forms, to name just a few: "Climate change. Ocean acidification. Dead zones. Oil 'spills.' Industrial fishing, overfishing, trawling, long lines, shark finning. Bycatch, bykill. Ghost nets. Deep-sea mining. Habitat destruction. Dumping. Radioactive, plastic, and microplastic pollution.

Ecosystem collapse. Extinction."[19] The wilder, more alien, and more awesome the animals appear, the less we have to notice just how far human activity reaches into their environments, and in many cases, into their bodies themselves, the fact that "at this point everything in the ocean has been touched by human practices."[20]

As pollutants bioaccumulate, the animals highest on the food chain are the most toxic. *National Geographic* reports that the oceans are a "toxic sink," and because many whale species are apex predators they serve as a measure of ocean ecosystem health.[21] In the BBC documentary *Planet Earth, The Future*, Payne, now founder and president of The Ocean Alliance, describes the very real way in which human activity lives inside whale bodies, in a statement which reminds us of that other thing we have in common with them: being mammals. In yet another cetacean entanglement, the breast milk of women in populations that rely heavily on a marine mammal diet, like the Japanese and Inuit, who eat whale meat, turns out to be very toxic.

> So for example, any woman of childbearing age, if she's nursing her infant in that tenderest of all mammalian acts, what she is actually doing is dumping her lifetime's accumulation of pollutants into that infant. And if her milk was in containers other than her breasts, she would not be allowed to take it over state lines, it's that polluted. We can dodge that bullet by simply feeding formula to our children; not an option for a whale.[22]

Not an option for a whale. These are precisely the same terms in which marine noise pollution is currently presented. The message of the recent documentary *Sonic Sea* is that the open ocean is an extremely dangerous place to all its animal inhabitants because of ambient noise. One of the speakers mentions that "the whales can't turn the volume down," invoking an image of invisible but deadly toxicity that invades lives and bodies, and which its victims are powerless to stop.[23]

Noise pollution is a very particular way to imagine an environment in trouble, a shift in frame from environment as that which lies outside the social to the complicated relationship between environment and society. Noise as pollution means that society always takes place in an environment, or that today's environmental problems cannot be thought in isolation from social ones. It is thus a powerful figure of how human impact on cetacean life is always necessarily both environmental and social, a perfect icon for the Anthropocene, in which crisis has become ordinary.

This is a lesson we learn from Lauren Berlant, who writes that crisis is no longer an event, but an environment. Unlike an event, which is "calibrated according to its intensities and kinds of impact," an environment "can absorb how time ordinarily passes, how forgettable most events are, and overall how people's ordinary perseverations fluctuate in patterns of undramatic attachment and identification."[24] Indeed, in today's environmental imagination, single catastrophes, which once signified much more powerfully in their own right, have been reduced to mere symptoms of more general and totalizing conditions like climate change and what conservationists call "collapse." Berlant zeroes in on the new banality of catastrophe, calling this situation "crisis ordinariness."

The very idea of noise pollution thus takes on the character of a kind of noise itself, ambient, inescapable, a new form of captivity. Killing us, but softly. Noise-related hearing loss in humans is a kind of slow death. Scientists are currently unearthing what's called "hidden" hearing loss in humans, and its attendant social effects, "hidden" because the threshold audiogram, the gold standard test of hearing function, can't pick it up. Threshold audiograms measure one's ability to detect tones in quiet, while noise-induced hearing loss concerns our ability to hear in noisy conditions.[25]

The Environmental Protection Agency reports that noise, not aging, is the leading cause of hearing loss today. National Institutes of Health classifies hearing loss as a communication disorder. Taking the more sinister implications of these combined claims to their logical conclusion, we can imagine a hearing loss (both material and "spiritual," for lack of a better word) resulting from the unbearable noise (material and spiritual) of contemporary life, a universal socio-environmental disease, as we succumb to the deafening din that irrevocably compromises the social. The whales can't turn the volume down. But neither, it seems, can we.

7 NOISE

Ambient marine noise due to shipping, drilling for oil, and Navy sonar has increased by a magnitude of two over the last sixty years. This means that for a blue whale that was born sixty years ago, the distance over which her vocalizations can travel and the vocalizations of others can be heard by her has decreased from 1,600 km at the time of her birth to 160 km at present.[1] As *Sonic Sea* shows, the mass stranding of beaked whales that occurred in the Bahamas in 2001 (17 stranded whales found over 36 hours) was due to Navy sonar, and many of the dead animals were found to have hemorrhages near their ears. Noise is causing not only deaths, but also less dramatic behavioral changes in marine animals that depend on sonar for their survival. Everything from migration patterns, to feeding, to mating is affected, and critics of marine noise consistently deploy the same word to describe the effect of human activity on marine mammals: stress.

Behavioral changes include changes in the vocalizations themselves. Recent studies of right whales show that they are literally yelling in order to be heard by each other. Biguenet's *Silence* ends on this note, as he describes reading a *National*

Geographic article from a few years back, in which he learns that right whales' social networks are getting obliterated by ship noise.

> I close the magazine and find the theme of the issue shouting in all capital letters at me from the yellow-trimmed cover: "POPULATION 7BILLION: How your world will change." But I'm still thinking about all those right whales vainly calling out for companionship in the noisy depths of the Atlantic.
> So what is the future of silence?
> More lonely whales, I fear.[2]

52 Blue has also been deepening his voice, and is now singing at closer to 47 hertz. And in this, he's not alone: blue whales as a species have been gradually deepening their calls since 1960, and shipping noise is one of the explanations offered for this change, although no explanation has been declared conclusive.[3]

How is marine noise imagined? Or rather, what are our limitations, as terrestrial, simian, seeing creatures, ourselves slowly losing our hearing, as we try to imagine cetacean auditory experience? In many pop representations, marine habitats continue to be depicted as "'alien' worlds, completely independent from human activities," as Alaimo writes.[4] This is certainly true in traditional visual representation, but not only. The recent shift to thinking about the sea in terms of sound conduction rather than sight seems at first to offer an alternative to this logic. *Sonic Sea* curates a specific auditory experience for the viewer, well-produced simulations of what whale song would sound like without ambient sea noise, saturated with reverb and encapsulated in the opening statement of the trailer, "Our ocean is a symphony where sound is the way of life, survival, or death."

And yet, the move to sound performs its own sort of alienation, because the visuals that accompany the sounds are already coded in particular ways. To simulate the dark and murky sea, in which hearing is the primary sense, the film routinely has the screen going completely black, with the marine sounds visually represented by animated multicolored arcs and squiggles, rushing ahead past each other and disappearing into the darkness. The experience is of a sort of enhanced hyper-hearing, what it might be like to inhabit the dark equipped with ears much more sensitive than ours.

The visual experience itself is a valuable insight into how limited our capacity to imagine marine environments really is. The difference between total, flat blackness and murkiness is precisely the difference that makes a difference. The black screen erases the fact that the dark murky waters of the deep sea are an environment in the first place. The sea becomes like space, the cold, empty vacuum of the astronomical imagination, rather than something material, worldly, worthy of being called a place.

Alaimo's critique of deep-sea photography in which abyssal animals are shown against a stark black background applies directly to *Sonic Sea*'s animated dramatization of whale experience: "The substance, agencies, and significance of the seas disappear. The dynamic liquid materiality is rendered a flat, static background, evident yet disclosing nothing. The backdrop belies not only the vast expanse of the oceans but the intra-acting material agencies of oceanic ecologies and human entanglements." The insight that sensing like a whale means seeing nothing and only hearing translates for us visual creatures into the well-worn myth that the sea is "an abyss, a nothingness, an immaterial zone separate from human incursions and transformations, and, thus, a sort of anachronistic space for the innocent pleasure of 'discovery.'"[5]

Following Lorimer, we might say that this kind of imagery seeks closure in conditions of unprecedented uncertainty. We are relieved of having to deal with the ocean as depth, both literally and figuratively, relieved of the pressures of how much we don't yet know, as "the given" is reduced to all the empirical data we need, presented against a dimensionless backdrop. We are relieved of murkiness, both material and epistemological, when in fact most of cetacean life takes place in murky water. Only in murky seas is it possible to discover a new cetacean species, as happened in summer of 2016, with a never before seen (and as yet unnamed) kind of beaked whale. The dead body had washed up on a beach in Alaska in 2014 and was misidentified as a Baird's beaked whale until two years later, when American and Japanese cetologists worked together and declared it an as-yet-uncatalogued species.[6]

It's of course extremely rare for a new large mammal species to be found on land, where visibility is not a problem. On one hand, because we are so ill-equipped to explore the ocean, we continue to discover its new large animals. On the other, it's for the same reason that we are discovering new species of megafauna this late in the game, as they are nearing extinction. Scientists have yet to see a living individual of the new unnamed beaked whale species. These marine discoveries are thus simultaneously exhilarating and ominous, reminders of how little we know and how much we are in the process of losing.

We are limited in our capacity to imagine the sea, but according to Alaimo, our incapacity to see the ocean the way we see land is actually promising and productive. The ocean "scrambles terrestrial orientations with aquatic immensities," she writes, not a "nowhere," but a profound displacement, an overtaking and undoing of terrestrial horizons.[7] Timothy Morton uses the ocean as a metaphor for any object, claiming that objects are impenetrable to reason because they continuously withdraw. In contrast, Alaimo challenges us to think the plenitude of the ocean, precisely as our thinking is undone by it. The ocean is not pure withdrawal from reason, and she would disagree with Morton that "depth is dark, absent from my (and anything else's) phenomenal space," insisting instead that darkness is not the absence of light or experience, but a color of its own, "unnervingly violet-black" or "the enthralling blue-black light."[8] Murkiness, too, is not the absence of the phenomenal.

Were the darkness of murkiness truly absent from my and anything else's phenomenal space, I could not be undone by it in the way Alaimo describes, enthralled, unnerved, falling into a *place* that continuously exceeds the terrestrial gravitas—and gravity—of that word.

Unlike the traditional conservationist demand that the only place worth saving is a place that we can experience as "somewhere," Alaimo invites us to reconsider the value of disorientation. Rather than thinking the ocean as some horizonless realm of pure circulation, we might imagine it in its full vulnerability, depth, and complexity, the terms in which writer, national park ranger, and wilderness activist Edward Abbey once described the desert, which he called "an oceanic world" in an effort to make readers see riches where there appears to be nothing.[9]

But there are other challenges to imagining marine noise. We have not yet figured out exactly how those capital letters shouting at Biguenet from the cover of *National Geographic* are related to the ship noise that results in lonely whales. And yet, because it has such profound social effects, noise as pollution is always more than auditory, what Michel Serres describes as "language garbage, . . . an audiovisual garbage that is so easily changed into money." Serres distinguishes between what he calls "hard" and "soft" pollution—the first being physical pollutants like chemicals, the second, "tsunamis of writings, signs, images, and logos flooding rural, civic, public, and natural spaces as well as landscapes."[10]

In contrast to Serres, Brian Thill deliberately doesn't distinguish between different orders of pollution in his Object Lesson, *Waste*. On the contrary, Thill's waste is almost metaphysical, a state to which everything, without exception, will eventually be reduced, except that different kinds of objects have different waste-like impact at different times. He uses the category "minor trash" in ways that capture both material noise and the noise of ideas under a single frame. Minor trash is, precisely, ambient. Describing plastic on beaches, Thill writes,

> It's often difficult to decipher exactly what each object used to be when it was part of something we thought we needed. The sense one gets when staring for a long time into these nests of plastic is that they belong to us and yet feel apart from us, because they constitute the planetary debris field we have scattered so thoroughly and minutely that it's hard to find anything particularly spectacular or notable in it. It is one of the many instances when seemingly minor trash demonstrates its immense strength and durability, having reached every corner of our planet and troubled or killed so many of the things it touches.[11]

Since hunting whales is against international law, the biggest threats to cetaceans currently are indirect and ambient, the minor made enormous, like climate change and human encroachment on habitat, threats that in the case of one cetacean species, the Baiji river dolphin, has resulted in extinction.

The Baiji lived in the Yangtze River. In the 1950s the population was estimated at close to 6,000. They were declared functionally extinct in 2006, the first cetacean species to have gone extinct as a result of anthropogenic factors, and the first megafaunal species to go extinct not from direct human persecution, like hunting, but from the "incidental mortality" resulting from environmental destruction. The leading explanation is unsustainable by catch in local fisheries, but noise has been singled out as another possible factor, since the Baiji, like all river dolphin species, are close to blind, relying entirely on their hearing. There is currently no river dolphin species that is not listed as endangered, and the vaquita, a porpoise resident in the Gulf of California, Mexico, is critically endangered, likely to meet the same fate as the Baiji's very soon.

It is thus premature to consider the Save the Whales campaign a success, just because some species returned to higher numbers because of the whaling ban. Blue whales are still listed as endangered. And perhaps most fascinating is how much we *don't* know about the cetacean scene: of the 90 cetaceans species that are known, 87 have been evaluated for conservations status, plus an additional 38 subspecies, and of those 125 groups evaluated, a whopping 49 are still classified as "data deficient." There are also, as we have seen, new cetacean species being discovered. But finding the as-yet-unnamed beaked whale in 2016 is hardly cause for celebration of the wealth of whales in our oceans. It proves not that marine biodiversity is increasing, but that it's simply (always) greater than we thought. And it is all under severe environmental threat.[12]

Sonic Sea ends on a hopeful note, indicating that quieter versions of all of the technologies that are presently interfering with animal sonar are available, and that it's just a matter of instituting them. At no point does the film question late capitalist development, the culture of growth, and its relationship to noise in general (not only marine). At no point does it ask us to consider how our daily lives, in which sustainability and upward mobility continue to be confused with each other, are connected directly to marine noise.

Our most basic desires for having the kind of life that counts as having a life, or what the first world calls "quality of life," is inversely proportional to the quality of whale life, if we consider that over 90 percent of the world's trade is carried by ship.[13] In its eagerness to show us the enormity of environmental problems in the seas, *Sonic Sea* turns away from the enormity of the social, terrestrial problems that give rise to the environmental ones.

What connections can we map between marine noise, literally speaking, and the "language garbage" of digital culture, most of which is images and written words? Cetacean entanglements, like all our entanglements with wild animals, are not merely about whales and humans. They are also about the communications technologies that mediate relationship among whales, among humans, and between whales and humans. At the moment, we might say there are at least three players in this game: whales, humans, and mass media, with the understanding that mass media is never just another player, but directs what forms of relation are possible, creating the rules of the game.

As pre- and post-Internet, respectively, for example, *Songs of the Humpback Whale* and 52 Blue are not only different sounds, they exist as products of fundamentally, qualitatively different social worlds: different modes of music distribution, imaginaries of collective experience, acceptable formats for social interaction, means of communication, understandings of what constitutes an environment, noise thresholds, visual engagement, and conditions of possibility for having a life.

We rely much more heavily on visual media now than when Payne released *Songs of the Humpback Whale*, with technologies creating more and more spectacular, complex, and sometimes even interactive viewing experiences. In contrast to *Songs*, which was a completely aural event, 52 Blue has very few actual listeners despite his great popularity. Given that his cultural significance is based entirely on his song, it's extraordinary that there is almost no interest in the sound itself. As we strain to connect to and through this vocalizing and acutely hearing creature, its sounds are no longer the point. The song of 52 Blue lives on YouTube, where the closest thing to an album is a small-scale project called "the loneliest mix." One can purchase the song custom-made by a guy on cassette, "one mixtape at a time," for six dollars.[14]

Unlike humpback songs, the sounds of 52 need to be sped up to be heard by humans, which may be the reason no one is rushing to produce the album, *Songs of The World's Loneliest Whale*. But shouldn't we at least have newer, "better" recordings of humpbacks by now? Numerous sources, from Amazon.com reviews to the *New York Times*, claim that *Songs of the Humpback Whale* contains the best recordings of humpback song available. It has yet to be topped. But why is this? Given the technologies available today, why has no one gone out of their way to produce the new humpback whale hit record?

8 WASTE

Meanwhile, contemporary popular environmentalism itself lives almost entirely on the Internet, nestled in between Facebook announcements of weddings, babies, home ownership and other signs of upward mobility, Instagrammed selfies, blogs about DIY projects, online shopping for expensive amino acids to regulate mood and high-end yoga mats, as the supportive quality of our social environment continues to lessen at an alarming rate.

In the US National Marine Sanctuaries promotional video, actor Edward James Olmos announces to the public that "now is the time to make your voice heard" about protecting oceans and coastlines, urging viewers to act both as individuals (each of us has a voice) and collectively (as participants in a democracy) to protect fragile marine environments.[1] And yet all of the media in which we are supposed to be heard are visual. As humans make their "voices" heard in the institutions available to them for what today passes for self-expression, the world becomes literally—visually—noisier and noisier.

As Serres points out, unlike hard pollution, which excludes because it is repellant, "the poster invites, calls you, and includes." The media understands and propagates noise by means of what he calls "noise technologies."[2] Films like *Sonic Sea* help us see the effects of material noise on animal lives, but the effects of the noise of ideas, or language garbage, are more difficult to isolate and show visually, especially as much of that visual media is itself already a form of psychic, sensuously powerful noise. How can we distinguish between the messages we wish to hear and the ones we don't when both come from the same "loudspeaker"? How can we reconcile the imperative to exercise our right to speak with the imperative whale song introduces, namely that we be quiet in order to hear it at all?

When Sylvia Earle, marine biologist and National Geographic explorer-in-residence, won the TED prize in 2009, she stated her wish in her acceptance speech (itself a TED talk): "I wish you would use all means at your disposal—films, expeditions, the web, new submarines—to ignite public support for a global network of marine protected areas, hope spots large enough to save and restore the ocean, the blue heart of the planet."[3] The more loudly we can speak about the destruction faced by the ocean and its inhabitants, the better. Indeed, the call to use our "voices" and use all the communication technologies available to us is the bedrock of conservationist culture in the Internet age.

As Earle speaks and the camera pans over the TED audience, overwhelmingly white and first world, politely tittering at her jokes and all apparently in agreement that this is what must happen, one cannot but wonder about the place of the ideas *industry*, in which TED is a leading player, in the production and spreading of soft pollution. How can we tell which ideas are truly "worth spreading" and which are simply garbage? And how should we navigate their entanglements?

Alaimo advises thinking about the dangers to marine ecosystems in terms of "the strange agencies of the ordinary stuff of our lives."[4] She means specifically the use of plastic, Thill's favorite example of "minor trash" which has such enormous impact. But the same warning applies to the agencies that result in noise, in both the sense of actual noise pollution and digital waste. Nothing is more *ordinary* than the desire for connection, and of course, nothing presents a more spectacular case of the ordinary expression of this desire than social media. The desire itself is so universal and innocent that the practices and affects it engenders in the digital age appear beyond reproach or even examination.

Decades before the Internet, Sagan was obsessed with the idea that the radio and television transmissions we have produced are floating through outer space, and that this "garbage" will reach alien intelligences long before Voyager does, causing the aliens to have the wrong idea about humanity. The 1997 film *Contact* (dir. Zemeckis), based on Sagan's novel of the same title, begins with a shot of Earth from within its orbit, the planet enveloped in a cacophony of its own radio sounds, dense, but full of identifiable snippets of late 1980's music, like the Spice Girls. As the camera pans out, moving away from Earth and past the outer planets of our solar system, the cacophony continues, and other snippets come momentarily into relief: REO Speedwagon, then "Funkytown" by Lipps Inc, followed by other recognizable disco, then the announcement that Robert Kennedy has been shot, then Martin Luther King Jr., then a sliver of Dean Martin singing "Volare."

We realize we are moving backward in the history of radio. The sounds quickly grow fainter as the sun recedes in the distance, hints of some Bing Crosby, then the announcement of D-Day, then a Maxwell House commercial and Judy Garland singing "Somewhere Over the Rainbow," and then a bit of "We're In the Money." By now, we are leaving the Milky Way. As this brief history of twentieth-century American culture via radio transmissions fades into complete silence, the viewpoint leaves another galaxy behind, and then another.

The takeaway is that the transmissions of the past are still out there, moving further and further away from us, "frozen in time" perhaps, but definitely not frozen in space. The *Golden Record* was to be a sort of corrective to all these accidental transmissions that were not meant for our alien neighbors. Sagan mused that "the launching of this bottle into the cosmic ocean says something very hopeful about life on this planet," an intentional antidote to our noise.[5]

Today, the question of what exactly we *mean* to launch into the ocean, cosmic or otherwise, seems to have fallen aside. Project DareWin is currently working on communicating with sperm whales, which have the largest brains of any animal, ever. They describe themselves as "an international group of audio engineers, scientists, cinematographers, authors, free-divers, and ocean lovers who believe cetaceans have an incredible capacity for intelligence and communication," and they provide the findings of their research on an open-source platform to anyone who is interested. The project is unique because the team is free diving in order to get close to the whales without scaring them off. Sperm whales swim away from humans in scuba gear because the gear makes noise (so much for Cousteau's "silent world"!). But when faced with quiet humans, the whales swim up close.

Journalist and DareWin team member James Nestor describes his experience of realizing that whale intelligence matches his own, using the terms we usually employ in this context, namely eye contact: "As I stared into the tennis-ball-size eyes of a sperm whale mother and her calf, I immediately recognized that these were extraordinarily intelligent, fully conscious beings. I believe the whales saw the same in us."[6] But this second claim is curious, given that we know that whales don't see very well. What's the source of Nestor's belief that the recognition is mutual, in the absence of the kind of data that arise from eye contact with other humans?

The whales emit two kinds of sounds. First the breathtakingly powerful echolocation clicks with which they "see" the humans, the loudest sound in the world and, according to the divers, fully capable of vibrating a human body to death.[7] And second, a soft flurry of clicks called "coda clicks," with which cetologists believe whales identify themselves to other whales. We can't know for sure, but it seems as if they are saying hello to a species they consider worthy of addressing, *pace* Lilly's conjectures that sperm whales might be utterly uninterested in creatures with such limited brains.

Fabrice Schnöller, DareWin's founder, attributes the success of their encounters almost entirely to the whales' own curiosity, about both the humans and the recording devices they wield. "That kind of extreme curiosity is something you would typically expect from only humans. But what I wanted to find out was whether their behavior was simply curiosity, or was there something more?" This "something more" Schnöller suspects to be a desire to communicate comparable to that of humans.

What has our response been so far? DareWin hopes in the future to develop something akin to Herzing and Starner's CHAT box, a machine that will capture the whale clicks, send them back to the animals, and see if they repeat them. "Next, the researchers will create artificial clicks containing three-dimensional sonographic images of things in our world—a tree, a human—and send these as well, prompting, perhaps, a kind of dialogue."[8] The hope echoes Herzing's prediction that "once they get it, things will go rapidly." But one has to wonder how intelligent beings would respond to a box making sounds it recognizes as its own, or for that matter, a sonograph of something as radically alien as a tree.

Furthermore, Schnöller's project suffers from considerable confusions of paradigm. On one hand, the newest sperm whale work suggests that each whale has a timbre to its click, similar to how each human has a distinct voice. On the other, Schnöller makes the ultimate move away from everything it might mean to be, precisely, a creature with voice. Unlike human communication, which he considers analog, "Sperm whale communication is digital. They transmit a thin sound with all the information contained inside it and then they can modulate it, a bit like the way the Internet works."[9]

And yet the need for intimacy burns as hot as ever. James Nestor writes about his DareWin dive that the discoveries made while listening were about connection. "This was an emotional epiphany, not a scientific one. That still means something." But then he gestures toward something quite extraordinary, namely the necessity of free diving: "You can't share that connection on the deck of a boat. You've got to get in the water."[10] For most of us, of course, a face-to-face encounter with the world's largest predator is not a realistic possibility for social interaction, and the desire for connection is addressed by consuming a lot of media. Because wild whale habitats are so difficult to access, the search for an emotional epiphany with whales often looks like surfing YouTube, posting to Instagram, maybe tweeting as 52 Blue about one's loneliness, yelling, if you will, over the din, adding one's own language garbage to the existing heap, or clicking "buy now" on one of the many possibilities for ever more remote engagement, including the new virtual reality content being created by DareWin specifically for use with Oculus Rift headsets.

If Sherry Turkle is right that the Internet is slowly shutting down our capacity to relate intimately, then environmental culture and digital culture make complicated bedfellows. Turkle describes online relationships as relationships "the way we want them," reminding us that offline relationships are unstable, destabilizing, unpredictable, and often painful: Love hurts, but not on the Internet. She argues that contemporary communications technology reveals, speaks to, but also produces "fatigue with the difficulties of life with people."[11] Dominic Pettman points out that while social media are inherently social (tautologically), "we encounter the now all too familiar paradox that *too* much media leads to anti-social situations, such as the proverbial friend or family member who would rather check their phone than talk to the people sitting at the same table. The social here migrates *away* from the directly interpersonal, to a simulated version with a much narrower bottleneck for giving and receiving social cues."[12]

Pettman writes that social media "teaches us to let go of personalized solicitations delivered via image, text, and sound. But it does so only to make ourselves newly available for the next distracting combination. And the next. And the next."[13] As with all consumption, however, as we let go of what we're done with, we fail to ask what happens to it once we're done. And thus these images, texts, and sounds become a sort of waste.

According to Thill,

> If we're all familiar with FOMO (fear of missing out), we're perhaps less familiar with what we might call FOTO (Fear of Throwing Out), but it's just as real and just as important. If FOMO was grounded in an anxiety that many of us felt in trying to keep pace with social media, online interaction, information and prestige economies, fear of throwing out is the other side of the coin . . . . It's not an instant nostalgia for the conversation flood so much as a kind of wake that our frenetic lives create as we move through them. But this wake lingers in ways it hadn't for earlier generations.

The lingering of digital stuff calls on us to become more and more sophisticated curators of "our daily process of emptying out our desires toward things over and over again." We end up remembering longer than our predecessors did, with their physical souvenirs and scrapbooks. It is becoming increasingly difficult to throw away the past and move on, as we haul our digital pasts behind us, "wanted and unwanted all at once."[14]

These are the strange, noisy agencies of the ordinary stuff of our lives, and they produce more and more waste, both physical and, in increasingly impressive quantities, digital. As we produce these mountains of idea garbage, the ineffable and silence continue to contract, as does depth of relationship and the very connection we in turn constantly seek. Understood not as the physical sound waves themselves, but the noise that makes it difficult to think, focus, and hear others, the noise of "content" degrades social life in perhaps the most abstract, undramatic, and thus most pervasive way. The ambience of waste. Minor trash.

If Schnöller is right that sperm whales are attempting to communicate with humans with the same degree of intention, curiosity, and care as humans are trying to communicate with whales, and if Lilly was right in making similar claims about dolphins, can such projects flourish in conditions of unprecedented noise? As both whale social life and human social life suffer, apart from each other, what dangers does noise pose for the possibility of a new collective, the vocal clan that would inevitably emerge in the course of multispecies communication work?

9 MUSIC

As of today, we still don't know why humpbacks sing. Because only males emit the most evocative (to humans) songs, it was long taken for granted that this was a mating call. Current research points away from this, since no female has ever been seen approaching a singing male, and new findings suggest that females might vocalize also. Recently, heartbeat-like, low-frequency pulses have been recorded in mixed-sex humpback groups off the coast of Hawai'i, and researchers speculate that they might be coming from the females. But the assumption continues to be that these are mating calls, as *Nat Geo* quips, "Who knows, maybe there could be a new track for *Songs of the Humpback Whale*: 'Let's Get It On.'"[1]

For Roger Payne, the comparison of humpback songs with human music is spot on. He explains on NPR that he decided the humpback recordings would put an end to whaling because it is criminal to "make cat food out of composer-poets."[2] "When I think of what grand arias, cantatas, and recitatives have filled the sea, echoing through its vast vaults, only to disappear and be lost forever, I am keenly grateful for those recorded by sound-pioneer Frank Watlington, who captured what I consider to be the greatest of all humpback whale performances, 'Solo Whale.'"[3] Performance, composition, poetry, opera, even the sea as a vaulted performance space with excellent acoustics—Payne finds all of these categories in the phenomenon of whale song without even a hint of metaphor.

With *Songs of the Humpback Whale* presented to the world as an LP, whale song was specifically addressed, destined to a listener, the listener of modern music. Indeed, the *Voyager Golden Record* positions its still-to-be-found alien audience the same way. But the kind of being that a listener is in this context is never examined. On the contrary, as speaking is imagined to be active and thus heavy with responsibility, listening is imagined as pure reception and passivity. Innocent. However, as Peter Szendy points out in his book *Listen: A History of Our Ears*, the listener (as opposed to someone who merely hears) is a product of Western art music, a complex construct of relatively recent human history.

Music invents the listener first of all by turning listening into an injunction: you must. Why would there be music at all, were it not because you must listen to it? But who is this creature that must listen? Szendy asks, "What place does a music work assign to its listener? How does it require us to listen it [sic]? What means does it put *into play* to *compose a listening*? But also: What scope, what space for *play* does a work reserve, in itself, for those who play it or hear it, for those who *interpret* it, with or without instruments?. . . . What is, as it is outlined and destined in the works, the *subject* whom music addresses, or rather the one it *constructs*? And what falls to this subject as something *still to be done*?"[4]

Edward Abbey once wrote, "Language makes a mighty loose net with which to go fishing for simple facts, when facts are infinite."[5] Reading Sagan, one gets the feeling that his project of communicating with aliens was never about what could be said in language, but about something much more intangible and abstract. His way of getting at the infinity of facts was not through language at all, but through music. What set Voyager apart and made it a more exciting project than the preceding pioneer probes was that for the first time

> we could send music. Our previous messages had contained information about what we perceive and how we think. But there is much more to human beings than perceiving and thinking. We are feeling creatures. However, our emotional life is more difficult to communicate, particularly to beings of a very different biological makeup. Music, it seemed to me, was at least a credible attempt to convey human emotions.[6]

For Sagan, as for sound studies pioneer Jacques Attali, music matters because it's "an instrument of understanding" the world, irreplaceable by any other we have.[7] Understood in this way, music is not opposed to language, but just another way of getting at what there is to talk about.

But why *is* music the way to get at emotions? And what is "emotional life," anyway? There's no simple answer to this. Lyotard attempted one, proposing a strange hypothesis toward the end of his life, one he himself knew was so speculative that he could make it only provisionally, even fabularly. For him, feeling and sound were intimately intertwined and at the heart of the problem of life itself.

He wrote that there is a sound without form, "both hither and beyond the languages of sound," that matter is at its heart sonorous, "but ultra- or infra-sonorous."[8] That there is something rather than nothing means that this something constantly laments its own passing. At bottom, life is lament and this is what the senses sense, or why there is sensation rather than nothing. Sound is death, or rather, life is sonorous because it's always dying and laments itself as loss. Sensitivity is this state of lament. Music, when it matters, sounds within the body the truth of matter as loss.

Thus, while noise and silence are mutually exclusive, music and silence collaborate. It is only through music that we can get at silence, the inaudible lament of the cosmos. Lyotard mused that for embodied beings, cosmic silence is only intelligible as a secondary moment, following the sounding of sound. Sound must come first, he argued. What else could the silence of space be for us, except music that has stopped playing?

Without music, how can an inaudible wailing be implicitly understood, how could it be imagined? It is a silent as the music of the spheres. They have no language and don't hear their own music. They wail on account of being cast into the void. The wailing of the cosmos is mute. Only percussion, beat, and discontinuity make it sing and allow for its terrible silence to be evoked after the fact.[9]

Lyotard grants his own hypothesis little philosophical value, realizing that the proposition is metaphysical, and for that reason suspicious and "hazy." He does not wish to maintain this as some truth about reality. His cosmological pronouncement is an attempt to understand why music moves us in the first place. He believes that the only place this inaudible lament of matter is available to us is in music. And importantly, it's not *in* the music itself, what composers call its "material," but in the "sonorous gesture that goes beyond the audible."[10]

This gesture is what distinguishes music from mere sound. All matter sounds because it howls the truth of death, of abandonment and passing, and music is music when it strives to let what is make itself heard. "Life laments its precariousness in an ever forgotten, anonymous death rattle. I maintain that music gets its beauties and emotions from the evocation of this condition of abandonment that is loud and mute, horrified, moist with a promiscuity without alterity."[11]

What do abandonment and lament have to do with moist promiscuity? This unlikely coupling is echoed today in the Hypersea hypothesis of biologist and geologist married-couple team Dianna and Mark McMenamin. *Hypersea* has little to do with the sea as we know it; it's the name they give to the land biota, both plant and animal, a distinction that falls away in their theory. When life moved out of the oceans and onto land, they argue, in order to survive, it took that sea inside itself in the form of bodily fluids.

The most awesome aspect of the land biota, they argue, is "that it vastly surpasses the marine biota in the physical connectedness of its constituents." Since organisms are primarily water, they can interact "at arm's length" only in water. On land they must touch in order to interact, and the authors argue that this makes marine relationships "seem sparse and platonic compared with the orgy on land."[12]

While the ocean itself doesn't interest them, the McMenamins imagine an orgy of fluids, for which bodies in contact are mere hosts, an ocean passing in between us that forces us to rub up against each other in order to maintain itself. As Vilém Flusser and Louis Bec put it, "Life can be regarded as drops of specialized seawater that eventually dissipate into unspecialized seawater."[13] The promiscuity of the terrestrial is thus an expression of life's precariousness. Not the sea around us, but the sea inside us. For the McMenamins, Hypersea is itself a kind of lament, an adaptation to an original displacement: our desire, a sign that we are not at home.

From this perspective, life as matter is indistinguishable from death. For Lyotard, matter is "the sound death makes in the living body. Or, again: the unheard sound that Being makes in the entity. Passibility or sensitivity opens the body up to trial. The latter is not an experience but an affliction."[14] When music moves us, it does so because it gives "voice" to this fundamental affliction, to the blow of loss that all sensitivity signals.

In other words, it's not that music expresses particular emotions, some "good," some "bad," but that it signals the condition for the possibility of emotions at all, aesthetic sense itself. Music—and for Lyotard this is true of all art—communicates the basic affliction of being embodied.

Thus, what one might call "emotional life" is really nothing more than the condition of being embodied, which means being vulnerable, violable. Being as dying. "The body is passible because it has doors and they are open. The same news enters through all these doors, always the same news— that it is not what it is, that it is nothing without affection, which nonetheless announces that it is nothing. What enters through the *blazon* of the body, sensations, *aesthesis*, is not just the form of an object, it's the anguish of being full of holes."[15]

Music, then, is not the "story" of our emotions, but a sort of document of life as essential penetrability. If simply the fact of being embodied is "the threat of being abandoned and lost," then music is the language of emotion only insofar as it announces this condition, this fundamental state in which horror is indistinguishable from desire, and the anguish of being full of holes is indistinguishable from life itself.

J. G. Ballard's short story "The Sound Sweep," published in 1960, is premised on precisely this idea. In a future in which some people work as sound sweeps, an occupation little better than a garbage collector, sweeping up audible sounds with the help of a machine called the sonovac, all sound has become noise, and thus waste. The world now enjoys ultrasonic music, delivered directly to the brain, unlimited by the constraints of the body. "Ultrasonic music, employing a vastly greater range of octaves, chords and chromatic scales than are audible by the human ear, provided a direct neural link between the sound stream and the auditory lobes, generating an apparently sourceless sensation of harmony, rhythm, cadence and melody uncontaminated by the noise and vibration of audible music."[16] The first casualty of this development turns out to be the voice, because no machine can produce it.

"In the age of noise the tranquillizing balms of silence began to be rediscovered," Ballard writes beautifully.[17] But ultrasonic music is not silence at all. The sound sweeps rid their environments of the noise of material music, voices, and other sounds, but the ultrasonic realm introduces an even broader spectrum of sonic experience. Thus, the key difference is not that one is quieter than the other, but that ultrasonic music is sourceless. Ballard's story shows a world in which music bypasses the material sphere and thus vulnerability itself. In this future, the experience of music becomes pure enjoyment of neural stimulation from nowhere, from no one in particular. It neither announces nor demands. Such a disembodied experience of music produces no anguish.

It was Payne's first wife Katy who discovered that the humpback patterns not only repeat, but also change. She credits this to her degree in music, not her other degree, biology. "It's sort of like jazz, she said, where each player riffs on the same methodical repetition, but innovates too."[18] It was the late sixties after all: not the quiet age of sail, but the golden age of jazz.

David Rothenberg has devoted his career as a musician and philosopher to playing along with different animal and insect sounds. He insists that whales are in fact singing rather than speaking and refers to whale songs as "art." His approach to whale song as music is very specific, placing humans and whales together in the Western avant garde, as when he writes, "Although we think we are always pushing the boundaries of what counts as music, humpback whales have been doing it for millions of years."[19] Elsewhere, he invokes John Cage in order to place whale song in the tradition of art music, inviting us to "listen to the interconnected patterns of sound all around as the strands of a vast natural symphony where overlapping intention forms the music of what happens."

And ultimately, himself a jazz clarinetist, Rothenberg invokes the great jazz soprano sax player Sidney Bechet. "He would practice scales and arpeggios for hours every day, but at the end of his sessions he would pause, and then launch into wild, shrieking animal sounds for the final minutes. A neighbor once asked him about this and Bechet responded, 'Sometimes I think what we call music is not the real music.'"[20]

For Rothenberg today both whale song and free jazz continue to be the real music. But because his specific form of engagement with whales is to not only listen to, but also to play to/with them, Rothenberg's accounts of what is happening elide between music and language, or rather, the distinction between music and language breaks down in his specific understanding of what it means to improvise with another being. His assumption that whales are creating sounds deliberately, spontaneously, and responsively banks on the idea that these sounds are communication of some kind, intentional enough to foreclose the loneliness that drives us (and, according to Eiseley, them) to seek out others in the first place.

"Most times when I drop my microphone and speaker underwater to play with the whales, I feel awfully lonely. There I am, making a strange sound and sending it out underwater, just hoping a whale might connect what he sings to what I'm playing. Often they just ignore me, but in the best of moments, and such a moment is just as rare as playing along with human musicians, some real contact may happen."[21] Whether whale song is language or music makes no difference in practice; what matters is "real contact," that frustratingly elusive thing that motivates all improvisation.

How does one know when contact is real? What does that look like? What does it feel like? The danger of romanticizing improvisation as some pure form of interaction is that this belief reproduces a popular misconception, namely that the improvising interlocutors are somehow being more honest, or more themselves, because the interaction is not scripted in the form of a composition. This is one of the most common misconceptions about jazz, that the sounds are utterly unique, spontaneous, and unprecedented, a sort of window into the musician's soul. What John Sutphen wanted echolocation to be, a form of x-ray vision into the mental states of others, many take improvisation to actually provide.

But a quick investigation into the nature of improvisation shows that it's not about communicational transparency. On the contrary, Jacques Derrida shows that improvisation can take place only in conditions of repetition and recognizability:

> It's not easy to improvise; it's the most difficult thing to do. Even when one improvises in front of a camera or microphone, one ventriloquizes or leaves another to speak in one's place the schemas and languages that are already there. There are already a great number of prescriptions that are prescribed in our memory and in our culture. All the names are already preprogrammed. It's already the names that inhibit our ability to ever really improvise. One can't say whatever one wants, one is obliged more or less to reproduce the stereotypical discourse.[22]

In other words, improvisation is recognizable as such only if it is, in a sense, scripted. The great avant garde saxophonist Ornette Coleman complained about this in an interview conducted by Derrida. Listeners assume that playing "free" is the same as playing "without following any rule," but

Coleman says the opposite is true. "People on the outside think it's a form of extraordinary freedom, but I think it's a limitation."[23]

Disappointing as this may be to those who pair improvisation with freedom, and counter intuitively, it's what makes contact possible at all. Derrida continues, "And there where there is improvisation I am not able to see myself. I am blind to myself . . . . It's for others to see. The one who is improvised here, no, I won't ever see him."[24] Because improvisation is possible only by means of the repetition of preexisting codes, there is no true self of the speaker/player to access at that moment.

It is not transparency and communion that makes contact possible, but recalcitrance and mystery. The "self" is accessible only to others, and not to oneself. Timothy Morton goes so far as to call improvisation "ecological" because it imagines different worlds, and is ruled by the uncanny encounter with strange strangers. When improvisation happens, Morton writes, we are not at home. Far from providing an experience of presence, or truth, or authenticity, much less anything like self-expression or the capacity to "be here now," improvisation is the fundamental breakdown of the self, the ground, and the world.[25]

Improvisation is thus irreducibly relational. No one improvises alone, except insofar as the self becomes split in two and one responds to oneself. It is at bottom a call to be answered by someone, even if no one answers in fact. Like Bechet's animal-like sax screeches, improvisation often sounds like noise, but unlike noise, which might be understood as sonic waste, proper to no one and cast away in the (vain) hope that it will disappear without response or echo, improvisation gets at something like music-as-call, proper to no one but a force moving through penetrable beings and demanding their attention to each other.

All of this would have sounded familiar to Sagan, who had his own take on the question of music and its place in the cosmos. He traced his passion for the Voyager project, and perhaps even for astronomy itself, to a "sound" that comes from no animal, namely the harmony of the spheres found in the work of Johannes Kepler. He even included excerpts of electronica artist Laurie Spiegel's piece, "Kepler's Harmony of the Worlds" on the *Golden Record*.

Kepler's hypothesis, dating to the early seventeenth century, was that physical harmonies exist in planetary motion. He found that the speeds at which planets moved around the sun corresponded to harmonies, positing real but soundless harmonies proper to each planet individually and to the relationships between them. Human music only mimics the original harmonies, which are expressed by the planets as they move around the sun, in a kind of choir, inaudible to creatures as limited as ourselves.

It seems at first that Kepler's interest was in mathematical order and equilibrium, but Sagan focuses on one of the strangest, least "scientific" moments of *Harmonices Mundi*. Kepler claimed that the speed of each planet corresponds to certain notes in the Latinate scale (do, re, mi, fa, sol, la, ti, do) and that Earth's motion corresponds specifically to the notes "fa" and "mi," which, he thus argued, the Earth was forever humming. But these are no mere notes; they stand straightforwardly for the Latin word for famine. As Sagan artfully explains, "He argued, not unsuccessfully, that the Earth was best described by that single doleful word."[26]

Ultimately, Sagan was transfixed by the idea that the hum of the Earth *is* its famine, its love song to the cosmos. The Earth itself as a cry, a massive message in a bottle, of which space probes launched by humans are merely tiny, flawed, rinky-dink emissaries. Not a mother, but more like a lover.

10 KISSING

Ingrid Visser is a marine zoologist in New Zealand, founder of the Orca Research Trust and the only scientist to swim alongside wild orcas while photographing them. Together with the orcas she has come to know well over the years, she has invented something, a form of greeting: when they see her boat, the orcas Visser knows immediately to swim up to it, at which point she sticks her face in the water and blows bubbles. The orcas respond by blowing bubbles back.[1]

Unremarkable, perhaps—were it not for the fact that orcas don't blow bubbles at each other in greeting, and that this is an interaction happening in the wild with no "reward" to motivate it except whatever is compelling about the event itself. One might object that the bubble-blowing orca is simply telling the human what she wants to hear, already locked into a codependent, intelligible, and clearly anthropocentric relationship in which domesticity kills desire and familiarity breeds contempt. But that the bubble-blowing orca happens to be aping the human at this moment is beside the point, because the bubbles "mean" nothing to either of them beyond the act itself. The activity is proper to neither species. What has been said when both parties are speaking the same language, but it's a language neither party knows how to speak? Nothing? Everything?

The greeting is the purest form of interaction. Essentially meta-interactive, it announces that interaction will take place, rules will be made, a relationship will be allowed to grow. Nothing is denoted, but the parties to the greeting have indicated to each other their desire to interact. They've shown interest. According to Haraway, the greeting is the most important part of communication. Her notion of "companion species" is about a relationship, something we do together rather than something we individually are or have.

This shift to the relationship as the smallest unit of analysis is necessary, she argues, because we are living in conditions of unprecedented interspecies toxicity and density. In other words, in a world in which using, killing, eating, objectifying, commodifying others, and being-commodity are no longer merely optional, a reality in which we can no longer be innocent, the individual can no longer be the focus of attention. Permanent complexity necessarily changes what counts as language, relation, and even truth telling.

There is no truth of the world prior to what contact between beings reveals. Reciprocal communication is not a matter of jointly describing a world that preexists the encounter. Interaction creates the world, and truth telling is something that can only be done together. It's in the greeting, Haraway would say, that something like truth takes place, as actors and world come into being as the ongoing products of relationships.

"This sort of truth or honesty is not some trope-free, fantastic kind of natural authenticity that only animals can have while humans are defined by the happy fault of lying denotatively and knowing it. Rather, this truth telling is about co-constitutive naturecultural dancing, holding in esteem, and regard open to those who look back reciprocally."[1] For Haraway, this happens between humans and animals, whose simultaneous similarities and differences to each other, vulnerabilities to each other, fear of each other, attractions and aversions to each other, dependency on each other, and (in)capacity to communicate with each other place them in a perpetual state of desire for connection. In other words, while it is ever more true that hell is other people, it is perhaps ever less true that there is no exit. The exit is also other people, and the people are animals.

It has thus always struck me that Ursula Le Guin's utopian classic from 1974, *The Dispossessed*, the ultimate science fictional treatment of the problem of how to live together, never mentions cetaceans.[2] The story's revolutionaries settle on a planet that has two seas, which are full of fish, but devoid of any marine mammals, much less cetaceans or anything that might readily present the problem of another intelligence.

The Odonian anarchists have long since been exiled to Annares, the moon of their home planet, Urras, from which they were banished. Urras is a planet much like Earth, covered by oceans and continents, while Anarres, their reward/ punishment for the revolution, is largely desert land except for two seas, and is devoid of animals except for fish, which are farmed as a major food staple. For generations, there is no contact between the worlds, so that the Odonians may build a new society from scratch, without Urrasti influence, beyond the reach of history.

The protagonist Shevek is the first Anarresti to return to Urras since the exile. He encounters animal biodiversity at the same time as he sees lush, green landscapes for the first time in his life. This is also his first time witnessing private property, marriage, poverty, abuse of power, wealth, oppression, gendered division of labor, and indeed, a society divided by gender. Besides the birds whose songs he hears at night in the city, his only real encounter with an animal is with his friend's pet otter. It's akin to his encounters with the wives on Urras—both are property, and both powerfully attract and repel him for that very reason.

Somewhere down the line, it becomes clear that the physical environment of Urras is intimately intertwined with the decadence and corruption of its society, and that the treatment of humans there is inseparable from the treatment of other animals. A rich, fragrant place, rife with injustice, inducing lust and, jealousy, Urras literally drives Shevek insane. Anarres, on the other hand, offers a rationalistic socialism, and freedom of sex and labor. But it offers these in a barren, sparsely populated desert.

It's as if Le Guin knew that in a world in which passions, drives, and attractions were seriously followed, and integrated with questions of justice, human and animal relations would have to be radically different than they are now, so different that developing this part of the story would distract from the human drama unfolding in her novel. So she created an environment in which intelligent non-human animals simply aren't a factor in the question of how society should be organized. The seas of Urras are home to otters, but there's no mention of other marine mammals. The seas of Annares are home only to fish. Whales remain silent in Le Guin's iconic work, perhaps because to include them would have resulted in a completely different story.

Utopian thinkers, a tradition to which Haraway arguably belongs, have known since at least the eighteenth century that changing the world required profound shifts in relationships between humans and other animals. Nineteenth-century socialist utopian Charles Fourier took the treatment of animals in his times as a symptom of profound social failure. Wikipedia credits Fourier with inventing the term "feminism," and upon closer inspection he turns out to have been not only the original feminist, but the original queer, interspecies, feminist thinker of labor, for whom labor is, at bottom, never-merely-human and fundamentally inseparable from desire, or what he calls "attraction."

Fourier argued that harmony was achievable, not only between people, but between all species, if we took seriously *the associative character of our social bonds*, understanding and following the laws of attraction that govern all life, including the material world. Only when we understood and followed attraction, he argued, would animals, people, and the material world become allied. Life would become immeasurably more beautiful. Only organization based on the laws of attraction could result in interspecies peace, and peace among humans was inseparable from peace in the natural world at large. The former couldn't happen without a major shift in relations with other animals and with capital-N Nature.

His favorite example of attraction leading to harmony involved the cochineal, a tiny beetle from whose body the dye carmine is extracted. The female cochineal produces carminic acid to deter predators. Dried beetle carcasses are ground to a fine, dark red powder, which is then mixed with different mineral salts, like aluminum and calcium, as well as with different citrus juices, to produce over twenty-five different renewable, non-toxic shades of red, from oranges and crimsons to fuchsias and profound violets. Fourier loved the cochineal not only because it brought color to the world, but also because of its usefulness to humans, which to him indicated preexisting attraction.

Red, of course, is not just any color. Rural Peruvian women have used cochineal for millennia not only to dye their beautiful yarns, but as a long-lasting, kiss-proof lip stain, and carmine dye is still a common ingredient in lipsticks.[3] Few things would have been more perfect in Fourier's imagination than the world that reveals itself in the kiss, when between mouths there is a thin layer of bright red lip stain dyed with acid extracted from the ground-up bodies of tiny beetles.[4]

The kiss returns as part of the utopian problem space in the *Golden Record* project. Ann Druyan was the project's creative director, and later became Sagan's third wife. The record includes an hour-long recording of her brainwaves, about which Wikipedia reports, "During the recording of the brainwaves, Druyan thought of many topics, including Earth's history, civilizations and the problems they face, and what it was like to fall in love."[5] Druyan also curated the "Sounds of Earth" section, in which she tried to show the whole of human experience in aural terms. During this process, she found herself surprised at how difficult it was to record the human kiss. Of the long catalogue of sounds the group amassed, she writes, "This wonderful sound proved to be the most difficult to record."

After numerous attempts, they still had nothing worthy of sending into space. But the reasons for this seem to have little to do with the sonorous qualities of kissing, and more to do with the social imaginary the kiss produces. "This was to be that impossible thing, a kiss that would last forever, and we wanted it to be real."[6] Druyan's almost mournful description suggests that perhaps the only desire greater than the desire to kiss is the desire that it be real.

Do whales have the same need? Whales don't kiss and don't even have what we would call lips. But they are the only other animals—besides humans—that mate belly-to-belly, or face-to-face. Of course, humans mate in many other positions, as well, but we are the only primate that mates belly-to-belly on a regular basis. Chimps are known to do so, but much more rarely.

Psychoanalyst Jacques Lacan once announced famously that there is no sexual rapport. Sex is our attempt to enter into a true union with another, a desire we can never satisfy. Still, it seems, we keep looking for sexual rapport. But so, it seems, do whales and dolphins. As all the other animals simply fuck, maybe cetaceans suffer like we do, from the (im)possibility of the sexual relation. Might the fact of their persistent face-to-face sex serve as evidence that they also long for the kiss to be real, so to speak?

Both Fourier and Lilly believed that such speculations about animal experience were necessary for the improvement of all social life on Earth. Fourier's approach to permanent complexity, was, like Haraway's, couched in considerations of desire, communication, delight, and imagination. All of these are traits that Lilly worried were in short supply by the second half of the twentieth century. "Sometimes I feel that if man could become more involved in some problems of an alien species, he may become less involved in his own egocentric pursuits, and deadly competition within his species, and become somehow a better being."[7]

Lyotard writes, "The only interesting thing is to try to speak the language of another that you don't understand."[8] But how do we do this? How can we speak the language of a creature, whose language we do not speak, by definition? How to begin?

This was the same question faced by Sagan and company in the *Golden Record* project. And while Lilly was not directly involved with the *Golden Record*, one of its producers, astrophysicist F. D. Drake, attended the now-famous 1961 conference on SETI at Green Bank, and reports that Lilly's dolphin work was at the center of how the goals and parameters of SETI were articulated, including "the equations that remain basic to the SETI problem."[9] Lilly was so popular at the conference that the attendees formed an informal group, "The Order of the Dolphin," which included the scientists who created *Golden Record* years later.

Large parts of Lilly's writings are dedicated to explicating the changes in attitudes on the part of humans that alien communication requires. All the beings involved (but especially the humans) would have to be "dedicated, courageous, open-minded, and knowledgeable, observant and quick, as well as kindly," and first and foremost, wildly, unprecedentedly imaginative. "It is going to require a great degree of imagination to empathize with such creatures. We must use our imagination and project ourselves into areas of which we have no secure knowledge."[10]

It's no wonder Lilly responded with such enthusiasm when Lovatt suggested the live-in experiment with Peter. Under the more general goal of two-way communication, the point of Dolphin House was to try something that had never been tried before: in other words, Dolphin House was not just the space for experiment, but an experiment in itself. An improvisation. Perhaps because this was a sustained and committed attempt at what David Rothenberg might call real contact, what resulted was nothing short of a scandal.

These days, no one remembers or cares much about the communication experiments themselves; readers both then and now are much more interested in Lovatt's admission that she routinely masturbated Peter to orgasm because there were no female dolphins for him to mate with. Although Lovatt herself thought of the act as necessary and just another part of getting to know Peter, it became a focal point for critics of Lilly.

Four years before, in 1960, Lilly and his dolphins had been on the front page of the *New York Times* (June 21). By the late 1970s, the publication most interested in the experiments was *Hustler*, which published a story about Lovatt without her knowledge, called "Interspecies Sex: Humans and Dolphins," as if the point of the experiment had been to study sexual relations between species. That, plus Lilly's interest in LSD (including experiments which involved injecting dolphins with the substance), topped off by the eyebrow-raising SETI, reduced the entire Lilly enterprise to an uncomfortable story of science gone wild, an interesting research program fallen prey to 1960s permissiveness.

In interviews, Lovatt insists that the genital contact with Peter was not a sex act on her part. A recent article in the *Guardian* calls it "innocent," and in Lovatt's lab notes she seems just as uninterested in the event as she is in this 2014 interview.[11] But the notes also describe another activity, a game that she and Peter invented that consisted of him running his open mouth (and thus his teeth) gently up and down the length of her legs, by which he had always been fascinated. "When we had nothing to do was when we did the most," Lovatt states. "He was very, very interested in my anatomy. If I was sitting here and my legs were in the water, he would come up and look at the back of my knee for a long time. He wanted to know how that thing worked and I was so charmed by it."[12] That the part of her in question was her legs indicated how well Peter understood the significant differences between them, almost like some tragic merman.

From these observation sessions, a spontaneous, new game developed, first involving a ball inside Peter's mouth while he ran just the tips of his open jaws along her shins. He later abandoned the ball as she allowed him to take her whole knee in his mouth. Lovatt was no longer afraid that he would hurt her, and she found herself murmuring to him softly throughout. "I had no idea of the end result of this play," she writes, but concludes that "this is obviously a sexy business," despite the absence of erection or genital contact of any sort.

Her description of it is unmistakably a story of a kind of seduction, one Lovatt can only convey by relying heavily on that well-worn tool for signifying ambiguity and anticipation, the ellipsis:

I had many fears. . . Peter obviously realized them and found ways, and props (the ball after all was a very convenient tool) to reassure me . . .. Peter continues pressing this game . . . and slowly I gain confidence. I no longer demand that the ball be there in the beginning of the game to make me feel better . . . . The mood is very gentle . . . still . . . hushed . . . all movements are slow . . . tone is very quiet . . . only slight murmurings from me. Peter is constantly, but ever so slowly, weaving his body around . . . eyes near closed.

Lovatt then speculates about Peter's motivations: "Perhaps this is his way of involving me in some form of sex play without scaring me away."[13] But Peter had no reason to think that Lovatt was scared of sex play with him, given that she routinely relieved him of his erections. It seems more likely that this was Peter's way of involving her in a form of sex play in which she herself was actually *interested*.

By her own admission, she was not scared when engaging in the other sex play with Peter, the one with a clear end result, but she also didn't think of it as sexy. The game with the ball and her knee, which she interpreted and experienced as some kind of sexual contact between them, was the one that fascinated her just as it did him. It was real, and the sexually mature Peter, however unlikely a suitor, knew the difference. Initially, Lilly presented Lovatt as Peter's human mother, but the description became inappropriate when it became clear that the two subjects were behaving more like lovers than like a mother teaching her child to speak. It is, as much as any love story, the embodiment of Haraway's dictum, "we are at stake to each other."[14]

Druyan's account of the attempts to record a real kiss includes one interesting detail: the group was "under strict orders from NASA to keep it heterosexual."[15] This is no surprise. The received wisdom for most of the world would have been—and continues to be—that the heterosexual paradigm is the true expression of universal human experience, from which everything non-hetero is taken to deviate.

The other woman on the *Golden Record* team was Linda Salzmann Sagan, Sagan's wife at the time. I like to imagine a different story, one in which the group fails to follow orders and two women share a kiss, which they send into the cosmos, bypassing Sagan altogether.

Perhaps the best framing of the relationship between Peter and Margaret may be borrowed from an interview with Michel Foucault from 1981, "Friendship As a Way of Life," in which he discusses what he calls a homosexual "way of life" in some unexpected terms. Homosexuality, which here stands in for any resistant sexuality, has to do not with a set of practices, but with the need for invention, or improvisation, he concludes. "How can a relational system be reached through sexual practices? . . . It can yield intense relations not resembling those that are institutionalized."[16]

Thus, such a kiss would have come closer to telling the story not of the human past, but of its future, a future in which humans greet their alien interlocutors. And that might have come closer to satisfying the team's desire for a kiss that was real. What's lost in NASA's orders is more than just the opportunity to represent a broader range of the forms human life can take. What's lost is the chance to treat the kiss as itself a greeting. Not the answer to the question of intimacy, but itself a question, intimacy *as* question.

"Friendship as a Way of Life" leaves us with an imperative: "We must think that what exists is far from filling all possible spaces. To make unavoidable the question: what can be played?"[17] While intimacy can only ever take us by surprise, this imperative reminds us that we can—and indeed, we must—create conditions for it to do so.

What can be played? In the end, the answer to this can only emerge from a sort of quiet.[18] Perhaps a listening or a waiting. Or listening *as* waiting, whether for whales or humans. But in any case, for each other.

ACKNOWLEDGMENTS

thank all the people who taught me about listening the hard way: by making music with me. Stan Killian, Clayton Dyess, Ray Wilson, Gerry Gibbs, Andy Langham, Hamilton Price, Bryan Copeland, Kyle Thompson, Clyde Adams, Mike Sjunka, Andrew Lienhard, Andrew Gordon, Mike Grebowicz, David Caceres, Gene Black, Phil Vieux, Chris Maresh, Eddie Hobizal, Matvei Sigalov, David Kane, Eric Kennedy, Jeff Reed, Bruce Saunders, Sheryl Bailey, Rogerio Boccato, Vardan Ovsepian, Joshua Davis, Rich Woodson, Mark Ferber, Ole Mathiessen, Josh Roseman, Ronen Itzik, Ben Monder, Ryan Ferreira, William Tatge, Tony Malaby, John O'Gallagher, Johannes Weidenmueller, Brian Charette, Maryann McSweeney, Pete McCann, Thiago Nunnes, Dan Weiss, Loren Stillman, and Matt Moran. This list is by no means complete. Special thanks to special supporters and audients Lindy Pollard, Joan Carroll, Aaron Goldberg, Gawain de Leeuw, Mark Lommano, Jon Heagle, John Rose, Scott Ellard, Julie Milgram, David Carr, my father, and a downtown jazz fan named Mark whose last name I never learned, who used to say about my singing, "She's on to something. It's not for everyone."

In May of 2015, Mark Ferber gave me a copy of that month's *National Geographic*. I was researching genetic modification of bees for a project with Dominic Pettman about libidinal ecology. The issue had a feature on genetically modified honeybees, but on the cover was a bottlenose dolphin. With Dominic's encouragement, that Fall I directed my libidinal-ecological framework to cetaceans.

On New Year's Eve 2015, Chris De Ville gave me his copy of *Ring of Bright Water*. Several months later, it turned out he had *Songs of the Humpback Whale* in his LP collection. We listened to it over and over that night. Chris Schaberg and I had been casually corresponding about airports, work, and life, and somehow it became clear to both of us at the same instant that whale song could be an Object Lesson. As Schaberg encouraged me to consider writing a book, De Ville presented me with *Lilly on Dolphins*.

The Occulture invited me to present parts of this at multiple Tuning Speculation conferences. Mackenzie Wark had invited me to speak about Donna Haraway's work on several occasions, and some of that material appears here. My mom and some of my friends sent articles in my direction that I ended up citing, including Greg Siegel, Eldritch Priest, Jacqueline Schlossman, and Dominic Pettman. Alice Frye took me to Cape Cod and accompanied me on a boat into the Stellwagen Bank Marine Sanctuary. My brother sailed from Alaska to Vancouver. Svitlana Matviyenko took me to Chernobyl. William Tatge took me to *Tristan und Isolde*. Jason Kruk took me to the salt mines, where it was very quiet indeed. The irrepressible De Ville made Negronis, cooked omelets, played records, edited the second draft, and indulged endless meditations on the nature of love, lust, loss, and the absurd, not necessarily in that order. And on New Year's Eve 2016, as if on cue, a humpback swam up the East River, one of over twenty individual whales sighted in the waters around New York City over the course of my writing year.

Such gifts. Thank you.

.

NOTES

Chapter 1

1 http://www.icb.org.ar/descargas/Songs%20of%20 Humpback%20Whales.pdf (1).

2 John Durham Peters, *The Marvelous Clouds: Towards a Philosophy of Elemental Media* (Chicago: University of Chicago Press, 2016), 66.

3 http://www.cbsnews.com/news/whale-song-a-grandfathers-legacy/.

4 The intermittent, distant dynamite explosions are audible on the recording, making the first song on side A, "Solo Whale," an eerie presentation of both sounds together.

5 Charlotte Epstein, *The Power of Words in International Relations: Birth of an Anti-Whaling Discourse* (Boston: MIT Press, 2008), 145.

6 Ibid., 105.

7 https://medium.com/@dealville/whales-synchronize-their-songs-across-oceans-and-theres-sheet-music-to-prove-it-b1667f603844#.u7y2xisha.

8 Epstein, *The Power of Words in International Relations,* 1.

9 Ibid., 89.

10 Carl Sagan et al., *Murmurs of Earth: The Voyager Interstellar Record* (New York: Random House: 1978), 13.

11 Ibid., 27.

12 Carl Sagan, *Cosmos* (New York: Random House, 1980), 287.

13 David Rothenberg, *Thousand Mile Song: Whale Music in a Sea of Sound* (New York: Basic Books, 2010), 4.

Chapter 2

1 https://read.atavist.com/52-blue.

2 http://www.odditycentral.com/animals/the-heartbreaking-story-of-the-worlds-loneliest-whale.html.

3 http://www.odditycentral.com/animals/the-heartbreaking-story-of-the-worlds-loneliest-whale.html.

4 Loren Eiseley, *The Star Thrower* (New York: Harvest Books, 1978), 43.

5 Sagan, *Cosmos*, 287.

6 Eiseley, *The Star Thrower*, 43.

7 http://www.smithsonianmag.com/science-nature/how-did-whales-evolve-73276956/?no-ist.

8 http://www.public.navy.mil/spawar/Pacific/71500/Pages/researchprograms.aspx.

9 For instance, see the *Audubon Field Guide to Marine Mammals* on the "loquacious nature" of Beluga whales, another toothed cetacean species, whom early whalers called "sea canaries" (318).

10 http://www.twu.edu/inspire/dolphin-therapy.asp.

11 Joan McIntyre, *Mind in the Waters: A Book to Celebrate the Consciousness of Whales and Dolphins* (New York: Scribner, 1975), 142.

12 John C. Lilly, *Lilly on Dolphins* (Garden City: Anchor Press/ Doubleday, 1975), 97.

13 McIntyre, *The Star Thrower*, 142.

14 Mette Bryld and Nina Lykke, *Cosmodolphins: Feminist Cultural Studies of Technology, Animals, and the Sacred* (London: Zed, 1999), 2–3.

15 Peters, *The Marvelous Clouds*, 68.

16 Lilly, *Lilly on Dolphins*, 136.

17 Peters, *The Marvelous Clouds*, 93–94.

Chapter 3

1 Vilém Flusser, *Writings*, trans. Erik Eisel (Minneapolis: University of Minnesota Press, 2002), 5.

2 http://www.whalesbermuda.com/all-about-humpbacks/ whale-behaviour/54-whale-song/66-humpback-whales-are-well-known-for-their-songs#The%20song%20of%20the%20 Humpback%20Whale.

3 Peters, *The Marvelous Clouds*, 59.

4 Lilly, *Lilly on Dolphins*, 25.

5 Ibid., 136.

6 Ibid., 197.

7   Ibid., 200.

8   Joshua Foer, "It's Time For a Conversation," *National Geographic*, May 2015, 53.

9   https://en.wikipedia.org/wiki/Context-aware_pervasive_systems.

10 Foer, *National Geographic,* 52.

11 Franz de Waal, *Are We Smart Enough to Know How Smart Animals Are?* (New York: W. W. Norton, 2016), 99.

Chapter 4

1   Although boredom has been suggested by scientists as the leading reason that cetaceans in captivity tend to do little on their own. See Gregory Bateson, *Steps to an Ecology of Mind: Collected Essays in Anthropology, Psychiatry, Evolution, and Epistemology* (Chicago: University of Chicago Press, 2000), 377.

2   John Biguenet, *Silence* (New York: Bloomsbury, 2015), 6.

3   Eiseley, *The Star Thrower,* 119.

4   Bateson, *Steps to An Ecology of Mind*, 371.

5   Ibid., 371–72.

6   Ibid., 374.

7   Ibid., 377.

8   https://www.newscientist.com/article/mg22129624-300-dolphin-whistle-instantly-translated-by-computer/.

9   http://www.technologyreview.com/featuredstory/532691/google-glass-is-dead-long-live-smart-glasses/.

10 Lilly, *Lilly on Dolphins,* 246.

11 Ibid., 217.

12 Jean-François Lyotard, *Postmodern Fables*, trans. Georges Van Den Abbeele (Minneapolis: University of Minnesota Press, 2000), 8.

13 Ibid., 61.

14 Vinciane Despret, "Thinking Like A Rat," *Angelaki: Journal of the Theoretical Humanities* 20, no. 2 (2015): 130.

15 Donna Haraway, "A Curious Practice," *Angelaki: Journal of the Theoretical Humanities* 20, no. 2 (2015): 5. My emphasis.

Chapter 5

1 http://www.theonion.com/article/dolphin-spends-amazing-vacation-swimming-with-stoc-33382.

2 Jamie Lormier, *Wildlife in the Anthropocene: Conservation After Nature* (Minneapolis: Minnesota, 2015), 38, 40.

3 http://www.earthtouchnews.com/natural-world/animal-behaviour/why-are-humpbacks-risking-their-lives-to-save-seals-from-killer-whales?utm_source=facebook&utm_medium=social&utm_campaign=article_humpbacks_orcas.

4 *Grizzly Man*, dir. Werner Herzog, 2005.

5 http://www.dailymail.co.uk/news/article-3612748/Why-decided-life-London-goat-Switzerland.html.

6 http://www.dailymail.co.uk/news/article-3612748/Why-decided-life-London-goat-Switzerland.html.

7 http://www.huffingtonpost.com/2013/01/23/cute-aggression-animal-cuteness-aggressive-behavior_n_2526909.html.

8 http://www.popsci.com/science/article/2013-01/science-says-adorable-animals-turn-us-aggressive.

9 Wherever investigators find abused children, they often also find abused animals, and vice versa. Rather than being endemic to all social life, both child and animal abuse point to the breakdown of the social fabric. See James Garbarino, "Protecting Children and Animals from Abuse" in *The Feminist Care Tradition in Animal Ethics*, ed. Josephine Donovan and Carol J. Adams (New York: Columbia University Press, 2007), 254.

10 Dominic Pettman, *Infinite Distraction: Paying Attention to Social Media* (Cambridge, UK: Polity, 2015), 18.

11 http://us.whales.org/blog/2016/02/we-should-stop-taking-selfies-and-start-looking-in-mirror.

12 Thom Van Dooren, *Flightways: Life and Loss at the Edge of Extinction* (New York: Columbia University Press, 2014), 4.

13 http://www.abcactionnews.com/news/world/rare-franciscana-dolphin-dies-when-plucke-out-of-the-ocean-and-paraded-to-tourists-for-selfes.

14 Donna Haraway, *When Species Meet* (Minneapolis: University of Minnesota Press, 2007), 75.

Chapter 6

1 http://www.ifaw.org/united-states/our-work/whales/meet-us-don%E2%80%99t-eat-us-campaign-take-whale-meat-menu-tourists.

2 Eiseley, *The Star Thrower*, 118.

3 Rachel Carson, *The Sea Around Us* (Oxford: Oxford University Press, 1991), 14–15.

4   Sagan, *Cosmos*, 5.

5   Stacy Alaimo, "Violet-Black," in *Prismatic Ecology: Ecotheory Beyond Green*, ed. Jeffrey Jerome Cohen (Minneapolis: University of Minnesota Press, 2013), 233.

6   Sagan, *Cosmos*, 5.

7   https://en.wikipedia.org/wiki/Space_debris.

8   Scott Russell Sanders, *A Conservationist Manifesto* (Bloomington: Indiana University Press), 102–3.

9   The same things that make the ocean mysterious from the terrestrial, that is, "walking," perspective make water recreation, especially SCUBA diving, attractive to people with mobility challenges.

10 Sanders, *Murmurs of Earth*, 96.

11 Lilly, *Lilly on Dolphins*, 222.

12 Gavin Maxwell, *Ring of Bright Water* (London: Longman's, 1960), vii.

13 See *The National Park to Come* and http://environmentalhu-manities.dukejournals.org/content/5/1/1.full.pdf.

14 Jamie Lorimer, *Wildlife in the Anthropocene: Conservation after Nature* (Minneapolis: University of Minnesota Press, 2015).

15 Ibid.

16 Bryld and Lykke, *Cosmodolphins*, 22.

17 William Cronon, "The Trouble with Wilderness" (1995), http://www.williamcronon.net/writing/Trouble_with_Wilderness_Main.html.

18 Bryld and Lykke, *Cosmodolphins*, 23.

19 Stacy Alaimo, "Oceanic Origins, Plastic Activism, and New Materialism at Sea," in *Material Ecocriticism*, eds. Serenella Iovino and Serpil Opperman (Bloomington: Indiana University Press, 2014), 188, 186.

20 Alaimo, *Prismatic Ecology*, 242.

21 http://news.nationalgeographic.com/news/2005/12/1213_051213_killer_whales.html.

22 "Planet Earth, The Future," BBC, 2006.

23 *Sonic Sea*, dir. Doughtery and Hinerfield, 2016.

24 Lauren Berlant, *Cruel Optimism* (Raleigh-Durham, NC: Duke University Press, 2011), 100–01.

25 https://www.sciencedaily.com/releases/2014/05/140507142804.htm.

Chapter 7

1 http://www.ifaw.org/sites/default/files/IFAW%20Australia%20%20Breaking%20the%20silence-how%20our%20noise%20pollution%20is%20harming.pdf. (4)

2 John Biguenet, *Silence* (Bloomsbury, 2015).

3 http://www.bbc.com/earth/story/20150415-the-loneliest-whale-in-the-world.

4 Alaimo, *Material Ecocriticism*, 188.

5 Alaimo, *Prismatic Ecology*, 241.

6 http://news.nationalgeographic.com/2016/07/new-whale-species/.

7 Alaimo, *Prismatic Ecology*, 244.

8 Timothy Morton, "X-Ray" in *Prismatic Ecology*, 321. And Alaimo, *Prismatic Ecology*, 245, 238.

9 (Abbey's desert was certainly not the same as Baudrillard's.) Edward Abbey, *Desert Solitaire* (New York: Touchstone, 1990), xii.

10 Michel Serres, *Malfeasance: Appropriation Through Pollution?* (Palo Alto, CA: Stanford University Press, 2010), 58, 41.

11 Brian Thill, *Waste* (Bloomsbury, 2015), 9–11.

12 http://news.nationalgeographic.com/2016/07/new-whale-species/.

13 https://business.un.org/en/entities/13.

14 https://www.youtube.com/watch?v=kJxuqLnr4OE.

Chapter 8

1 http://sanctuaries.noaa.gov/#HI.

2 Serres, *Malfeasance*, 45, 75.

3 http://www.ted.com/talks/sylvia_earle_s_ted_prize_wish_to_protect_our_oceans?language=en#t-1004474.

4 Alaimo, *Material Ecocriticism*, 188.

5 http://voyager.jpl.nasa.gov/spacecraft/goldenrec.html.

6 http://www.nytimes.com/interactive/2016/04/16/opinion/sunday/conversation-with-whales.html?emc=eta1&_r=1.

7 The DareWin divers claim that this hasn't happened yet only because the adult whales are so conscious of their size, and that they simply choose not to kill the divers. http://www.bbc.com/news/magazine-29209139 and http://www.bbc.com/earth/story/20161206-the-people-who-dive-with-whales-that-could-eat-them-alive.

8 http://www.nytimes.com/interactive/2016/04/16/opinion/sunday/conversation-with-whales.html?emc=eta1&_r=1.

9 http://www.bbc.com/earth/story/20161206-the-people-who-dive-with-whales-that-could-eat-them-alive.

10 http://www.nytimes.com/interactive/2016/04/16/opinion/
sunday/conversation-with-whales.html?emc=eta1&_r=0.

11 Sherry Turkle, *Alone Together: Why We Expect More From
Technology and Less from Each Other* (New York: Basic Books,
2012), 10.

12 Pettman, *Infinite Distraction,* 31–32.

13 Ibid., 48.

14 Thill, *Waste,* 32–34.

Chapter 9

1 http://news.nationalgeographic.com/2015/12/151207-
humpback-whales-sounds-noises-oceans-animals/.

2 http://www.npr.org/2014/12/26/373303726/recordings-that-
made-waves-the-songs-that-saved-the-whales.

3 http://www.whalesbermuda.com/images/stories/Reference/
Frank_Watlington_and_the_whale_song.pdf.

4 Peter Szendy, *Listen: A History of Our Ears,* trans. Charlotte
Mandel (New York: Fordham University Press, 2008), 7–8;
author's emphasis.

5 Abbey, *Desert Solitaire,* xii.

6 Sagan et al., *Murmurs of Earth,* 13.

7 Jacques Attali, *Noise: The Political Economy of Music,* trans.
Brian Massumi (Minneapolis: University of Minnesota Press,
2009), 4.

8 Lyotard, *Postmodern Fables,* 220.

9 Ibid., 230.

10 Ibid., 230, 218.

11 Ibid., 226.

12 Mark and Dianna McMenamin, *Hypersea: Life on Land* (New York: Columbia University Press, 1996), 4.

13 Vilém Flusser and Louis Bec, *Vampyroteuthis Infernalis*, trans. Valentine A. Pakis (Minneapolis: University of Minnesota Press, 2012), 33.

14 Lyotard, *Postmodern Fables,* 230–31.

15 Ibid., 231.

16 J. G. Ballard, "The Sound Sweep," in *The Complete Short Stories* (New York: Norton, 2010), 93.

17 Ibid., 92.

18 http://wvtf.org/post/it-took-musicians-ear-decode-complex-song-whale-calls#stream/0.

19 http://opinionator.blogs.nytimes.com/2014/10/05/how-to-make-music-with-a-whale/?_r=0.

20 https://orionmagazine.org/article/serenading-belugas-in-the-white-sea/.

21 http://opinionator.blogs.nytimes.com/2014/10/05/how-to-make-music-with-a-whale/?_r=0.

22 Jacques Derrida, "Unpublished Interview 1982," http://www.derridathemovie.com/readings.html.

23 Jacques Derrida and Ornette Coleman, "The Other's Language: Jacques Derrida Interviews Ornette Coleman," *Genre* 37, no. 2 (2004): 320.

24 Derrida, "Unpublished Interview 1982," http://www.derridathemovie.com/readings.html.

25 See Timothy Morton, *The Ecological Thought* (Cambridge, MA: Harvard University Press, 2012).

26 Sagan, *Cosmos*, 64.

Chapter 10

1 Donna Haraway, *When Species Meet* (Minneapolis: University of Minnesota Press, 2007).

2 Very little sci-fi has been devoted to the question of human/cetacean relations. David Brin's *Startide Rising* and Vonda McIntyre's *Superluminal* both take this on in different ways, but both focus on the technoscientific adaptations that would be necessary in order for such interspecies life and communication to become possible. Brin presents a universe in which species "uplift" other species to higher levels of intelligence. Humans have uplifted dolphins, among other species, and are traveling through space on ships manned by human-dolphin crews. McIntyre presents the opposite, an Earth on which some humans have been genetically modified to be able to live in the ocean and communicate with whales. What neither story seriously explores is how deeply the question of relation in general would be troubled by such new couplings, how disoriented "the social" itself would be, apart from the machinations required to achieve these interspecies collaborations.

3 https://www.youtube.com/watch?v=FXbYFn0vg3U.

4 Carmine dye is also used, less romantically but just as flesh-to-flesh, in pancolonic chromoendoscopy, to help detect cancerous lesions in the colon.

5 https://en.wikipedia.org/wiki/Ann_Druyan.

6 Sagan et al., *Murmurs of Earth*, 157.

7 Lilly, *Lilly on Dolphins*, 207–08.

8 Lyotard, *Postmodern Fables*, 61.

9 Sagan et al., *Murmurs of Earth*, 47.

10 Lilly, *Lilly on Dolphins*, 19.

11 https://www.theguardian.com/environment/2014/jun/08/the-dolphin-who-loved-me.

12 https://www.theguardian.com/environment/2014/jun/08/the-dolphin-who-loved-me.

13 Lilly, *Lilly on Dolphins*, 178–79.

14 Donna Haraway, "Tentacular Thinking: Anthropocene, Capitalocene, Cthulucene," *e-flux* 75, September 2016, http://www.e-flux.com/journal/75/67125/tentacular-thinking-anthropocene-capitalocene-chthulucene/.

15 Sagan et al., *Murmurs of Earth*, 157.

16 Michel Foucault, "Friendship As a Way of Life," http://commoningtimes.org/texts/mf_friendship_as_a_way_of_life.pdf, 137–38.

17 http://commoningtimes.org/texts/mf_friendship_as_a_way_of_life.pdf, 140.

18 Foucault was not exactly famous for his sexual asceticism, to put it mildly. And yet, what follows from his position is precisely a sexual and cultural ascesis, however strategic and temporary.

INDEX